"James Langteaux's daring new book, *Gay Conversations with God*, is one written "for such a time as this." This is a time when a deluge of grace and truth purges the earth of religious pretense, hypocrisy, and intolerance, and all the captives are set free to be finally themselves just as God made them.

Everything that can be shaken will be shaken, and Langteaux fearlessly shakes things up here with unflinching clarity. . . not just as a gay man who has been there and done that in the world of high profile Christian media, but as one who speaks with the provocative tone of a prophet. Someone needed to say these things—to boldly go where no one has gone before…"

—Bishop Jim Swilley, Church In The Now, Now Ministries

"This book will **definitely** not make the Baptist Women's Book Club list. . . However, this is a must-get-out-there book! I am a reading snob and I loved it!"

—A Pastor [who wishes to remain anonymous]

"James Alexander Langteaux is an incredibly gifted, poetic writer who pens words so beautifully that I'm moved to tears and impassioned to love every time I read them. I am convinced that Jesus Loves Homos! And that message is far more important than you or me."

—Jeremy Casper, Filmmaker

"Christians were once known as witnesses to God's love and grace—those who kissed lepers and welcomed strangers. Somehow we've morphed, acquiring a reputation for judgment, especially condemning those we've exiled as 'unclean.' I suspect it's because we're much better at telling than listening. For those ready to give one of our own a turn, I would invite you to hear James Langteaux's heart. Suspend the need to be right for a moment and truly listen. Jesus is not ashamed to call him 'brother,' just as he is. Neither am I. Please hear his story, his pain, his faith. Read this book."

—Brad Jersak, Author of *Kissing the Leper*

"In my own search I discovered that I could never offend God while I was being honest with him; in fact, I find that he urges me on to tell it like it is. This has helped me to discover (in process) who I am and that it's OK to be me. And this is what I now read within the pages of James' new book. I applaud his honesty and wit and I hope that *Gay Conversations with God* encourages many people to ask the same questions of themselves."
—Chris Falson, Singer/Songwriter

"We look at other people's lives through our own filters and often miss the complexities of who they are in themselves, in God. James strips away those filters applied to him by others and lets us into the humor, the pain, the struggles, the lies and the victories. For those of you who think God is only in the tidy places with the heterosexuals, *Gay Conversations with God* will bother, challenge and enlighten you. And, in the end, I hope it confronts the filters in which you may wrap the other children of God. There is freedom in Christ, for all of us."
—Kathy Baldock, Canyonwalker Connections/Str8apology

"After reading *Gay Conversations with God*, I went out today with a smile and so much joy! Suddenly I knew that God loves me— and that made all the difference. In my closet where I was hiding from myself were guilt and shame and the belief that I was unlovable. James' story is one of sacred tenderness and acceptance. At times, as I was reading, I knew I was in truth, listening to the voice of God. How real and honest the words are. James has such a poetic gift as a writer . . . simple and deep and embracing and real!"
—Toni Gilyard, Poet/Author of *the girl between the trees*

Gay Conversations
with God

green press
INITIATIVE

"This logo identifies paper that meets the standards of the Forest Stewardship Council. FSC is widely regarded as the best practice in forest management, ensuring the highest protections for forests and indigenous peoples."

Gay Conversations with God

Straight Talk on Fanatics, Fags, and the God Who Loves Us All

James Alexander Langteaux

FINDHORN PRESS

First published by Findhorn Press 2012

ISBN 978-1-84409-582-7

British Library Cataloguing-in-Publication Data.
A catalogue record for this book is available from the British Library.

Cover design by Andrea White
Author photograph by Aaron Gautschi
Edited by Rachelle Gardner
Layout by Thierry Bogliolo
Printed and bound in the USA

Unless otherwise noted, all scripture quotations are from the *The Message*
by Eugene H. Peterson. © 1993, 1994, 1995, 1996, 2000. Used by permission
of NavPress Publishing Group. All rights reserved.

Scripture quotations marked "KJV" are taken from the *King James Version*
(public domain.) Scripture quotation marked "NIRV" is taken from
the New International Reader's Version, © 1996, 1998
by Biblica, a Colorado non-profit corporation.

Published by
Findhorn Press
117-121 High Street
Forres IV36 IAB
Scotland, UK
t +44(0)1309 690582
f +44(0) 131 777 2711
info@findhornpress.com
www.findhornpress.com

For Twyla

For God so **loved** the world
that He **gave** His only begotten Son,
that **whosoever** believes in Him
should not perish but have everlasting life.*
John 3:16 (KJV)

*Some restrictions may apply.
See participating church for details.

Contents

and wishes down . . . so the one you love can rise above
and live in the fullness of their calling and dream.

With or without you.

Preface

I remember the day James first revealed the original title for his book. "It's called *GOD HATES FAGS and Other Bedtime Bible Stories*," he said. "Do you think it's too risqué?"

I, a rebellious and free-spirited 21-year-old at the time, responded, "It's perfect!" He decided to test some of this daring new material on a captive audience: the What Club, a speak-easy James had created, a place for artists and misfits to congregate, share, perform and get a little tipsy.

As James stepped onto the stage to read an excerpt from his bold new work, I could tell he was extremely nervous. His brow "glistened" and his voice and hands trembled slightly. He knew his words would be polarizing . . . but something was driving him, possessing him almost, to go far beyond his comfort zone (already a rather spacious place). As James finished his reading the crowd began to applaud and gradually they stood up and cheered raucously, as any dazzled bar crowd would. Now, many years and revisions later, James Alexander Langteaux's book is finally in your hands (or maybe on your "device"), new title and all.

James and I have laughed, cried, gotten terribly drunk and shared many intimate stories over the last 15 years. But I must admit, even I found several parts of this book uncomfortable to read. "What was he thinking?" I often thought to myself. Was he really ready to reveal this much of himself to the world? Surely the religious right would find it nothing short of blasphemous and the QLGBT and liberal people I know are hardly interested in having someone else's view of "God" explained to them.

But as James says, this book poses more questions than it offers answers, and "a man with an experience is never at the mercy of a man with an argument." That's what this book is about. An experience. And it is one that many of us have shared. Not down to the fine details, of course, but all who have felt ostracized by religion have at some point pondered, "Am I really unloved by God? Why would any God create me, only to condemn me?" And it's this confusion, I believe, that prevents many a misfit from pursuing a quest for a higher power.

This book is James's story of how he made peace with himself and his God on this very quest. It captures the hurt and frustration many of us have felt on this journey. It also offers the reader the opportunity to share in the loving and acceptance of not only ourselves, but a power greater than ourselves.

If anything, I hope you come away from this book with a sense of relief that not everyone shares the viewpoint of those religious whackos on TV. But more importantly for those of you still struggling with the guilt and shame of your own religious upbringing, this book may well be your ticket to freedom.

—Sam Sparro
Musician & Recording Artist
October, 2011

The

Foreskin

(A little bit more than Foreword)

If you are circumspect, I'm now giving you the choice to be "born-again." You can trim this extra bit, but it's more authentic if you leave it in. This time it's a choice *you* get to make.

This may seem like a bit of irrelevant extra material—but it offers a modicum of protection before you become over-stimulated by the incendiary words to follow. For some this may be a little much to swallow.

You can cut this out or you can roll it back—or you can play with it before you proceed. You can choose to ignore it but if you do, then don't blame me for your disease. Let this odd little pre-ramble serve as a warning!

This book is not politically correct, and it will offend those of you who are. It will, without a shadow of a doubt, cost me my inheritance and alter the rest of my days here on earth. It is a veritable dick slap to the big business we call the Christian church.

I've written two "*Christian books*," I've hosted *Christian shows* and I even worked on the studio floor with Pat Robertson for nearly five years on the *Christian Broadcasting Network*.

But playing strip poker with the big wigs in Christianity today while hiding the gay card up my sleeve is a game I no longer wish to play. The stakes are too high, not because *they* may find out the "truth" but because it is causing me to withhold the **real Truth** from the big world outside the little Christian Ghetto—a cloistered community of closet cases and dangerous religious thugs who keep warning us over and over about the dangers of using drugs. Meanwhile they use religion as an opiate to dull the minds of the masses, while they milk the poor unsuspecting slobs who make up the lower classes.

Queer Christianity

I have traveled the world interviewing young people in pubs in Prague, under the stars on the stairs of Sacre Coeur, on the windwashed moonlit beaches of Mumbai, on broken walls in old war camps on the Russian border and on the Orient Express from Istanbul to Vienna. In nearly every single conversation Christians are described in the exact same way with almost no variation.

Here's what the critics are saying:

> "Christians are narrow minded, judgmental,
> bigoted, hateful, homophobic, hypocritical bad
> tippers with a hidden agenda to get me to join
> their church."

Funny, Jesus said his followers would be known by their **love**.

Lost in Translation?

I don't know about you, but if the Christian brand represents those things to our world today, then I don't want to be a Christian anymore. I want to be known by my love, not my hate, I want to be in relationship with the One who made all my brothers and sisters while I learn to love them just the same.

I don't want to be part of the mega-church country club and be a pastor of great renown. As crazy as this may seem, I want to blow the walls of the churches down—in a non-terrorist sort of way. (Pardon my Homeland Insecurity) Then with the rubble of those walls that separate us from them, I want to take the broken pieces and build bridges to broken men.

Confessions of an
X-Christian
I'm born again *again*

It is time to tell the Truth about the God who allegedly hates gays. It's time to tell the Truth, because, quite simply, there is no time to tell it any other way.

If you are religious, do not buy this book.

Please pray for me instead.

If you are politically correct or easily offended, then for the sake of us all, go do everything possible to keep the constitution from being amended.

But if you are a fuck-up who is sickened by hypocritical, narrow-minded bigoted Christian buffoons, who insist that to find God's love there is something first you will have to do . . . then this is an imperfect book for you.

I know for a fact that this is definitely a book for me. For the writing of these words has been instrumental in helping set me free. As THE great teacher once said while he walked among the right and religious, the very ones who ultimately pegged him to a tree:

You will know the Truth.
And the Truth will make you free.

The ever loving subversive, and true revolutionary
—J.C.

1.
Welcome to Wisconsin.
Smell our dairy air!

I have loved God for as long as I can remember. And I have loved the boys that he created for the very same amount of time. Despite the fact that many insist that our sexual preference is a choice, I would have to say that of all the choices one can make in the land of the free and the home of the brave, choosing to be gay would have to be one of the stupidest choices one could make. At least that was the case before *Will and Grace*. Believe it or not, there is a choice that is even more insane: The choice to embrace the Christian God while admitting to the congregation that you are not exactly straight.

Oh Good God, Heaven Can Wait!

I believe there are lots of things that just sort of happen to you, things you have absolutely no control over—like who your parents are and where you happen to land right outside the birthing canal.

Speaking of where you land, being gay while believing in God is a little like being from Wisconsin: nobody asks for it to happen to them, and you never admit to it—unless the person you're talking to is also a cheese head. And you try like hell to find the fastest way out, desperately making the best of it while you are there.

My earliest memory takes me back to an old barn somewhere in the heart of "America's Dairyland" where I "milked" my first boy at the wizened age of five. Maybe I was four. I don't remember.

There in an abandoned stall filled with fifty-year-old cow shit, I talked Nicky Hartman into taking his pants down while he played the role of the cow. I'm not sure of my inspiration for the act, as I didn't actually live on that farm, and I had never seen a boy or a cow milked before, but I milked the piss out of little Nicky Hartman, pulling firmly and furiously on his little wiener, filling a plastic Cool Whip container nearly to the half-way point. Little Nicky then became the farmer, and I topped off that flimsy forefather of the Tupperware line.

A reoccurring Dream Whip™

Nicky was a nervous little kid by nature and although he was shaking during the process I could tell that it was an anxious mix of fear and adrenaline fueled by pure excitement.

His little mentally challenged sister, however, wasn't quite so easy. She watched from the next stall, begging for her turn to be next, but for the life of us, we didn't know how to milk a girl. Girls were foreign, their equipment was hidden and besides, we didn't have much interest in exploring the scary world of girls' anatomies.

But the bellering little nuisance cried so loudly that we finally let her pee in the flimsy plastic dish (without our mechanical assistance) to avoid an unnecessary visit from our parents. It was a competitive world in the non-dairy farming arena and our agricultural secrets were to remain ours and ours alone.

Got Milk?

I'm not sure where nervous Nicky is, I don't know if he turned out gay, I'm not even sure if he's alive today. But I am sure of one thing. We were fucking amazing farmers, Nicky and I. Not much demand for our piss poor product, but I enjoyed the fresh air while working in the great outdoors and the feeling of accomplishment that comes when you work with your hands, making something out of almost nothing. (We were five, okay?)

Ours was a simple and sheltered life growing up in the Midwest. Thank God we didn't have to face the perversions of the big city.

Lord knows where I would be today.

From the Bovine to the Divine

I'm going to fast-forward over a lot of details from my early years, mostly because I can't remember them, and partly because they're not at all interesting. Suffice it to say that I was the only child of a broken home. My mom worked tirelessly in her beauty shop to keep food on the table and plastic drapes on the windows of our tiny apartment in Abbotsford, Wisconsin. I was left to fend for myself from as early as I can remember. A man who was dating my mother (the man who later became my stepfather) once asked my mother where I was. "I don't know," my mother replied. "I think at Rosie's Bar having lunch."

I was four at the time.

(An A.D.D moment that makes me fidget)

Some of the memories are now coming back.
I invited a little person over for a sleep over—
a little person who was in eighth grade and I
was only eight. But he was my size and to
me, that was great. (My mom didn't think
so. She stayed up all night at the top of the
basement stairs watching to make sure that
this little man didn't take any liberties with
her little boy.) I was fine. And so was my little
friend who seemed to enjoy the homemade
chocolate chip cookies . . . except he wasn't
allowed to smoke or call his bookie.

My story, however, is definitely no *Running with Scissors* kind of
tale, even though I was often the outsider. I was the creative only
child who was always new in town, suspect and different even
though I had lived there for years. I guess little kids have keen gay-
dar and just know that you're queer. And that often translates to:
"You are not welcome here." So instead of playing football you
sing in the choir. You eat and eat to your heart's desire, gain lots of
weight, experience hate, start lifting weights, (now you're looking
great), you take the stage, engage the crowd, excel academically
and be the class clown. You keep them distracted, make sure
they're all laughing, do whatever it takes to keep them at bay— all
in an attempt to hide the fact . . . that you're gay.

Despite being the outsider for as long as I can remember, I look
back fondly at my early and involuntary declaration of independ-
ence and realize God often seems to know what he is doing . . .
preparing us perfectly for our tailor-made journeys that lie ahead.
If we can only make it through the madness, endure the hate, the
hurt, the shame and sadness . . . if we can tolerate and survive the
neglect, the rejection or abuse . . . we often find that even the most
painful of experiences can prove to be of use. They prepare us, sea-
son us, soften us and make us more compassionate to those who
have endured things we may not have or behave in ways that we

don't appreciate or understand. It is often the wounded who ultimately become healers and it is the wounded who tend to know how to feel. It is the wounded who are most likely to fight battles on behalf of the misunderstood and we fight with tenacious fervor and zeal.

Welcome to the desert of the Real

Or, at the very least, welcome to my faltering journey toward finding comfort in my own, often ill-fitting skin and welcome to God's broad field filled with Calla lilies and grace. Though you may not be comfortable reading every line or chapter and there may even be places where you flagrantly disagree, I hope you'll find this book is worth the read.

Because while digging for diamonds in a life filled with shit, you often discover what you truly believe. And that has to be worth something, maybe even $19.95 plus tax. If not, perhaps I can send some of your money back.

But this is not to be confused with a guarantee—just me suffering with another bout of tangential A.D.D.

2.
Tears for Queers.

Give me *Liberty Middle School* or give me death!

(Wait, I think they are one and the same.)

I'd just finished mowing what seemed like acres of lawn in the balmy humidity of late summer in the Midwest. Teenagers were somehow made responsible to maintain the oversized lawns created by feudalistic parents who secretly harbored aspirations for the gardens of Versailles—undoubtedly in an effort to outdo the neighbors.

Greenest Envy

I rinsed the itchy grass clippings off in the shower before I settled comfortably next to my stepfather on the couch to watch the nightly news. It was sort of a family tradition in my household. My mother would be working away in the kitchen, sort of listening when the blender, food processor and other assorted kitchen gadgets didn't interfere. Needless to say, she had a stuttered take on world events. Then again, don't we all.

I was thirteen or fourteen at the time, wrestling with that awkward transition between boy and man, with a body that was slow on the uptake making gym classes nightmarish at best. It seemed the other boys had grown hair in all the right places years before me and their dicks seemed to have tripled in size overnight. I did a lot of surreptitious meat gazing in the locker room, pining for the day when my tiny twig would grow up to be a strapping sapling with ample foliage like the other boys.

These were the farm boys, who brilliantly attributed my lack of development to my "city slicker" status—as if a village of 1500 in the middle of America's Dairyland could possibly be confused with fashionable urbanity. Was it the damn fluoride in the water that kept my willie looking wiry or was it the lack of backbreaking farm work that stunted my growth? Maybe shoveling shit and yanking on teats would have done wonders for my whacker—I would never know.

I wish I would have known then what I know now. These were not flaccid cocks . . . staring me down in that dank, vomit colored shower room. These boys were at half-mast, ready for what, I'm not exactly sure. I can only guess.

Erector Set

Many of my male classmates, the jocks for the most part, were my enemies. They were suspicious of boys who checked out other boy's packages in the locker room—all the while they themselves were sporting "semi's" in an attempt to add length and girth to somehow enhance their self-worth. All these almost hard-ons in a steamy, sweaty, testosterone charged basement of our middle school made for quite a confusing sexually-charged milieu.

"Damn it, Kurt, if you wouldn't work yourself up into near porn-star proportions, I wouldn't be staring." I wish I would've had the balls to say it to the boy who openly accused me of being gay, his openly aroused penis swinging freely as he fished for a jockstrap in his gym bag. Thank God he had something to hold that thing back. If anyone should be accused of being a faggot in the locker room, logic would dictate that it would be the
"boys in
the wood."

I honestly think that those traumatizing days in the junior high gym somehow fed into my sexualizing of the male body. Granted, I had an attraction to boys from as early as I can remember, but these moments only solidified the overall fascination.

I wanted to know what it felt like to have that much meat . . . that much girth and length in my hands. I fantasized about what it would be like to work with Stephen Grabinski's junk. He had play-girl perfection going on, and it was hard not to imagine what it would be like to be in Stephen's shoes—or better yet, in his briefs.

Details @ Eleven

The fact that I subscribed to *GQ* and *Details* at an early age didn't help my cause. I was fascinated by the social life in New York, the flamboyant fashions and the beauty of the young models who somehow knew my secret, but didn't seem to care. It was their secret too. And I suspected that these beautiful demi-gods endured their share of torment in high school basements by their classmates and coaches alike. But they made it to the other side.

Although I hate to say this, much less commit these words to print, I would love to emasculate Rod Stuttler with a dull Mexican road worker's machete. A fuckin' idiot gym teacher, he favored the athletic boys while taunting those of us who needed nothing but help, encouragement and grace to make it through those awkward transitional years and even more awkward and mandatory post P.E. showers. If Rod had been trained to teach, I'm guessing his certificate had a watermark in the shape of a Swastika.

If it wasn't bad enough to be called a fag by an ignorant jock with an oversized cock and an undersized brain, it was sheer hell to have a paid faculty member ridiculing my lack of ability in dodge ball, when I could undoubtedly write circles around him—a faculty member who was being paid to babysit boys playing games in cavernous gymnasiums echoing with screams, screeching whistles, and bouncing balls.

Since most of the jocks at school, and any male faculty member who taught in any sub-intellectual capacity (shop class, gym class, or coaching) openly identified themselves as my enemy, it became all the more troublesome to learn that my stepfather aligned himself with the Anti-Gay Gestapo—making the enemy too close to home. Making my home a frightening new battle zone. I had nowhere left to go.

This Just In

As we watched the news, the incredibly rare story involving some form of homosexuality was brought to our attention by Ted Koppel or Walter Cronkite. Inwardly I was uncomfortable having the topic talked about openly, but maybe a little relieved to know I wasn't the only freak in the world. Prior to "GRID" or the Gay Related Immune Deficiency, now known as the AIDS epidemic, almost no one talked about queers. Except for my peers . . . with barbed words that nearly brought tears.

At least on the inside.

Just when I thought we had made it through this uncomfortable report, my stepfather, the man who taught me about the love of Jesus, the man who helped me know a God of love, suddenly broke the most startling news to me about strange and violent glitch in God's big plan. Just as my Mother brought dinner out and just before we joined hands . . .

to pray

. . . without blinking, he looked directly into my soul, and with a smile that even Jack Nicholson would be envious to capture for his most twisted of roles, he shared a new gospel with me. It wasn't turn the other cheek and it had little to do with the virtues of being meek. Venom dripped from each word that fell from his tongue-talking mouth.

"Fags should be lined up against a brick wall and mowed down with a machine gun!"

He waited for my response.

"Really?" I said with a telling quiver in my voice. "That seems a bit harsh, don't you think?" I tried to sound diplomatic while maintaining an air of disinterest to distance me from those God damned queers and fags. Those heartbreaking names I heard nearly every day—that sometimes still echo through my mind's hallways—filling me again with fear, self-loathing and shame.

"You sound defensive," my stepfather accused. "Are you one of them? Are you a fag?" I may have sucked in gym, but I flourished in my academic pursuits and I was smart enough to remember the ample gun cabinet in the basement before I responded. "I'm going to my room."

"What's the matter, are you some sort of fag?" he sneered. Walter or Ted warned about growing tensions in the Middle East but I wasn't concerned. I couldn't even eat. My home was suddenly riddled with land mines. War had been declared by yet another man who should have known better, who should have loved better . . . who could have helped this confused, awkward boy-not-yet-a-man navigate the horrific seas of puberty with a measure of understanding and grace rather than a healthy serving of blood lust and hate.

The sound of machine guns ripped through our den. Menachem Begin had determined that the Gaza Strip was worth the price of countless men. Over bloody images of dead Palestinians and Jews, Jimmy Carter was pleading for a cease-fire and an end to the bloodshed—right when my stepfather had called for more.

I now had a taste of what it was like to be unsafe in my own home—to be wished dead by enemies, classmates, coaches family and (perhaps, the greatest betrayal of all) sometimes even myself.

And that's the way it is
August 18th 1979.
Good night.

3.
Behind
The Sins.
A Glimpse into the Dark
and Lonely Closet

I will never forget the day when the insanity of my world finally came into complete focus. I was working with the script for a show produced by the *Christian Broadcasting Network*, dealing with the *triumph over the struggle of homosexuality*. It was early evening and I had put in another long day in the studio. Our 6:45 a.m. production meeting always seemed to begin seven minutes too soon and my excuses for being late were casually ignored when I presented a white bag full of fresh warm bagels. I learned early on that distraction was better than deception.

Every morning the senior producers gathered to plan the format for the live *700 Club*, which aired in millions of households worldwide. The day was now far spent and the golden hour had long since passed. I was alone scripting the host's dialogue and a series of questions for our X-gay guest who would be on our Sunday version of the "Club." I kept checking my watch hoping that I would still make my dinner date.

Just when I thought I was going to make it home in time, one of Pat Robertson's security men knocked at my office door. I was tucked away in a corner in the attic, where the "Gen-Xers" on staff had carved out a unique little world of our own. My heart jumped at the sight of this unexpected visitor and I feared the worst. Though I had done my best for years and years to honor God and sleep with no one even though I was queer, I had grown tired of the battle and even more exhausted by being alone *and* saddled with guilt. So for the first time in my life I had decided that it may be okay to live in a way that was true to myself, and I put my fear and reservations high on a shelf. The only problem was, you never knew when someone may find out. And when you work for Christian Nazis who want an easy bake oven to take care of the fags—you can never, ever feel safe—not even on the very top floor.

Suddenly security was outside of my door. I had been found out and this was going to be my exit under the cover of darkness in the company of a security man. Much to my surprise, the security man was actually a boy riddled with insecurity. After an awkward hello he stood quietly for what seemed like an eternity before he finally broke the silence with the revelation that he was gay and was going to have to leave his wife and maybe his post.

He had tears in his eyes as he stood shaking behind me. I turned from my computer to face him. "Welcome to the Club, my friend. I know exactly what you're going through. I'm writing a show on the transforming power of Jesus for homosexuals and I'm worried that I'm going to be late for dinner with my boyfriend. Isn't life crazy?"

A smile broke through his storm. "I want you to remember something, Brian. *You are loved.* Nothing will separate you from God's love. Nothing. Don't ever forget it and don't let anyone tell you otherwise." Brian seemed to take some solace in my words.

And despite the fact that I was quite convincing, I remained unconvinced.

According to the security man, his honesty cost him dearly. His wife, also on staff, alerted the higher-ups and this young, warm-hearted, God-fearing soul was escorted from the premises like a common criminal. This was a man who was finally willing to come clean and tell the truth and his reward was a healthy serving of shame. I learned from Brian's mistake. I learned how to play the game. And I convinced myself that I wasn't a fag. I was something else. Something better and more enlightened—very deconstructed and free. I was not going to be tethered by stereotypes and I wasn't going to accept any labels or wave any rainbow-colored flags. I could love people—men and women alike. It so happened that I preferred to sleep with men exclusively.

But I wasn't gay.

Sixteen long years have gone by since that strange meeting in the upper room. I have been on a long and dangerous journey fighting a silent war with myself. I have lived believing that I can be "set free" from this struggle, and I have lived in abject despondency—believing that nothing would ever change. I couldn't fully enjoy either the world of hedonism or the world of ministry and I was unable to give myself to anyone unreservedly because the landmines and grenades would go off when I least expected.

It was never safe to simply "be." I was trying like hell to please God while I denied myself. And I have finally come to the place where I know that I will never please God until I am truly honest with myself. Jesus said, love your neighbor as you love yourself. That means you must first love you—before you can *ever* love anyone else.

Well.

All these years later, I think I have finally found a broad field of freedom, and for the most part, it is landmine free. I've let go of all the things I've been told and I'm allowing the God of the Universe to speak to my soul and love me—just as I am.

And I am.

Loved.

And more than that, I am finally free to fully be the man I was created to be . . . a man among men who happens to love men. And these are words I never dreamed that I would say.

I am God's son and I am gay.

So by speaking out and sharing my journey with you, I'm not attempting to prove that homosexuality is not a sin. (If I were going to write *that* book I would have done so when I was 21 and hot.)

This is simply a journal that chronicles a stuttered journey toward whole . . . one that I hope gives glimpses of God's incredible, undeniable, irrefutable, unfathomable love. I have always believed that a man with an *experience* is never at the mercy of a man with an argument. This is my experience, my rites and wrongs of passage, written in an insane fashion to welcome the reader—gay, straight or anything in between—into the crazy world of "believe."

Because you actually have to enter it
before you can ever see it . . .

The world's wisdom says I will believe when I see. God's foolishness says: believe and you will see. Faith is a funny pursuit. She often dances alone in the shadows, just out of reach. But when she welcomes you into a slow dance, there is nothing more sublime than to rest your head on the sweet shoulder of her embrace.

And after all these years I think I am finally able to believe.

God is love.

And I am free to dance in the warmth of that love. And in the words sung by Marlo Thomas, a thousand years ago, spinning on a little dung-colored turntable in my third grade classroom—a well-crafted lesson that was sung over and over to me and all of my friends . . . a lesson I wish I would have learned way back then . . . a lesson that would have enabled me to live so much differently . . . a lesson that has finally spun its way into my soul from that scratchy 33 . . .

"And you and me are free to be you and me."

4.

Coming Out. (A Little)

A long time ago in a galaxy far, far away, I came out. (A little).

Don't get me wrong, it was a pretty bold move on my part and I will not negate that fact. From the age of about nine or so, I wanted to publish a book, more than anything else. While all the other kids were playing doctor I was making my friends play "author" and sit in our basement in front of an old cast-iron potbelly stove with antique typewriters. There in that idyllic literary space I would insist that we come up with brilliant pieces of literature.

The old adage is, write about what you know. And since most prepubescents don't know much about life or love, we had to pretty much make shit up. We would sit and type by the fire for hours while the wild Wisconsin winter winds whipped the wind chill deep into the double digits of the subzero region. I would then insist that my poor mother edit, retype and send my horrifying manuscripts off to Houghton Mifflin or one of the other big publishers of the day. I had more rejection letters at age 12 than most people may ever have in a lifetime.

So back in 1999 when I was finally offered a book deal with a major international publisher (and it was quite by accident, I might add) I was ecstatic. I remember the elation and the pride that sort of carried me off in a rapturous tide.

It all went along swimmingly until God sort of interrupted the heady process by asking me to come out.

Now, one significant fact to keep in mind is that this was the very, very conservative Christian imprint of said major publisher—and to the best of my knowledge, no one had ever come out in a Christian book before. At least not in the way that I thought God was leading me. It is also important to note that this wasn't to be a "coming out" story. This particular book was all about hearing from God and trusting him enough to do what he says—at any and all costs. So, it would've been disingenuous of me to hear God ask me to come out—and then ignore his voice when I'm asking the reader to respond to whatever God asks him to do.

And I was no fool. I knew that if I obeyed him on this one—the entire book deal would fall through. It would all be over before it even started and it was all because God asked me to tell a secret that the Church at large, does not want to hear.

They are so sure that
God must hate queers—

So after years and years of trying to keep my sexual orientation a secret from everyone—apart from the ones I wanted to sleep with—I suddenly found myself facing the horrifying prospect of putting it all in print.

And for a Christian audience.
(This was a gladiator moment. No Lion)

And so I wept. Then I would sweat. I was begging God to change his mind because I really did want to see that book make it into print, and so far it was a book I believed in because it was all about belief. Belief in the God that loves us with all his heart—the God who wants us to be in relationship with him—and trust him when he asks us to do crazy things. Things that may cost us our lives. Or, at the very least, our reputations. (Or our book deals.)

So I finally relented. And I did come out . . .

a little.

I told the world in the chapter 8 of *God.com* that I had finally fallen in love with someone incredible, and God had asked me to give that person up. I went on for pages about the pain of that separation and how I thought I would never recover—and yet I didn't mention a gender or a name—and I didn't plan to. Ever. Then God interrupted my writing and asked me to come clean. To me this proposition alone seemed beyond obscene, because it would mean the end of my writing dream. Reluctantly, I wrote chapter 8.5 which boldly proclaimed in 155 point font:

I Am A Hypocrite . . .

And there it was—only a sentence or two—this shocking revelation requiring so few words, only that my love had a man's name.

If you blinked, you might have missed it. And some people did. But for those that God had intended to see it, it was quite revolutionary and it caused a few thousand people to write me and tell me secrets of their own—and thank me for letting them know that they weren't alone.

The problem was, I made it seem as if the problem had been only this one person that one time and even though I insisted that the publisher allow me to print the words "I am not fixed"
I somehow assumed that in my honest and public revelation, God would bring me to a place of freedom from that horrible life of shame.

I figured that in obeying God's crazy request for transparency and putting even that little bit into print, there would be this astounding angel chorus that would lilt into my writing room in the mountains—and a supernatural occurrence would carry me off to the land of the straight and narrow where I would no longer be consumed by the desire to spend all my free time with men.

Naked.
And ashamed.

I believed that somehow in my act of honesty I would be set free from homosexuality and it would only be a matter of time. I also knew that I had to do this as God had let me know, years and years before, that he was building a platform for me and I would not be able to take my place on it until I was completely honest. Honest with myself and the world and be willing to identify with "my sin."

If he, a sinless being, was willing to identify with *all sin*—and yet I was not willing to be identified with the "sin" that I did commit— then in essence I was saying that I was better than him. (Oh, activist reader, would you please wait before you go all ballistic here with the term "sin." It will all be a little more clear in the chapter entitled "Sin Tax.")

So I figured this was it. That this would be the place where I would walk out on the platform that God had prepared for me—

The only problem was, I hadn't identified with being gay—I was only telling the world that I had a single gay relationship but then I walked away. I didn't mention all the others. I didn't mention the fact that the attractions never left. They only intensified.

And it would have all been so much easier if I had only died.

Not come out. A little.

So, here we are, years and years later, in another place and another time. Ironically I'm writing on a cruise ship in the Caribbean—we are at port somewhere and I'm sitting outside the floating casino with a window facing the sea—writing these words to you today with nothing but joy in my heart. Not angst. Because I can only give thanks to the God who has been so patient with me—the God who was willing to see me through those tiny little baby steps of faith that could bring me to this place today.

It is a journey, you know.

I am excited to see what these words of honesty and truth will do. I'm excited to hear what happens to you—after you read these words and let them settle into your heart and mind. Because I know for a fact that God will do something spectacular if you only give him time.

And I know for a fact that if you are willing to believe—and if you are willing to be honest, God will show himself to you like he has shown himself to me.

This is probably the most exciting journey that I have ever been on—and I'm not talking about the ship. I'm talking about this bold journey of living in transparency and in truth—in a willingness to freely admit to who I am and, at the same time, fully understand that

I
    AM
        LOVED.
            Just as I am.

And so are you. If you are married with children but you are secretly gay . . . you are loved. If you are hiding so deep in the closet that you can't even say the words to yourself . . . you are loved.

If you are burning down the house because you are the most flaming queen the world has ever seen . . . you are loved.

(Probably loved flamboyantly!)

If you are the big bad leather daddy bear covered in all your glorious hair . . . you are loved.

No matter who you are or what you are into . . . you are loved.

I am certain of that. I am certain of this one thing—that God has a love that transcends our understanding for his sons and daughters, all types and all kinds.

He has created us to be ourselves and to be willing to improve ourselves, where it is needed. And if he wants or needs to change anything major about you or about me—*he* will do it, because it is impossible to do it any other way. As it turns out, God is the one who brings life to the dead. The corpse, it turns out, has little say. I am powerless over most of the messier things in my life. But I am finally starting to understand that God can and will change us in the areas that he sees fit. For instance:

I was a chain smoker. That chain is broken.

I was a pre-alcoholic (maybe saying that alone,
negates the "pre"). Whatever the case, I now control the alcohol, it doesn't control me.

I used to be a self-loathing closet case and now I
am a strident fag and what's more I'm actually
happy and gay—and I don't give a damn what
the right and religious have to say!

Change is possible if we are only willing to put our hand in his
hand and believe.

It really is that simple.

And there is no greater place to be than out of the closet and into
the light of his love—dancing freely in the sun—and allowing the
world to judge—or not judge—and still not have to hold a grudge.
Because it does not matter.

(What you think of me is really none of my business.)

There will always be haters. It is our job not to hate but to allow
ourselves to let go and forgive. And in so doing, we will truly live.
And it is my guess that we will be living cancer free—because
there is no longer any bitterness, anger or jealousy coursing
through our healthy hearts and beautiful bodies.

This is the beginning of a brand new day. A day where we can be
the sons and daughters that we were intended to be—

And the best part of it all is that we can be free.

(And he who the Son sets free, is free indeed.)

I'm coming out a lot in this book. And I'm inviting you to do the same. And on the outside of your stuffy little closet filled with the balls of moths—you will find the love of God—and the love of so many others it may take you by surprise. It may even blow your mind!

I know now for a fact that the writing of this book was essential. Even if it does nothing for you at all.

Because sometimes it is a matter of telling the truth—that sets a larger truth in motion—a truth even larger than this huge old ocean that we are currently cruising on—and that Truth may do something across all space and time—something so powerful and so sublime—and we may never even see the results in our brief lifetime.

Take a chance. Tell the Truth. Live in the Truth and then receive the love of the Father that is yours for the taking. No matter what anyone else may be saying.

You are loved.

And, what's more—there is a big welcoming world, just outside of your closet door.

5.
Fucking
Hard.

Okay.

Here's the deal. I'm sorry that I'm about to offend some great people.

In general, I don't mind being offensive. I'm quite gifted in the area and I've had years of studied practice. My motto has always been, "I'll burn that bridge when I come to it."

I should probably also admit that I've never been one of those "keep in touch" type people. I used to make a lot of promises—feverishly jotting down email addresses and phone numbers, even street addresses back in the day when that actually mattered. I'd nearly stumble over myself as I promised to call or write and send expensive gifts on all the appropriate occasions. People tended to believe me. I know I did.

As much as I wanted to be a "keep in touch" person, my problem is, I live too much in the moment. I try to give myself to the person I am with—completely. And when I'm with the next person I try to do the same. Even though the last moment may have been spectacular. If you dwell on it—and write everything down in your journal and jot down everybody's contact information—there is a good chance that you are going to miss the next moment.

You can't bottle great moments. And when I've tried to relive them with someone, I find the carbonation is gone and the conversations always seem to fall a little flat. I think that may be because of the expectations that you carry into that next meeting. There is no way that it can live up to the magic of what was . . . because you didn't expect it the first time.

The fact of the matter is—you can't keep in touch with everyone. When I was growing up, my parents used to tell me that if you have one or two good friends you are a lucky person. I always thought they said that because they were not very good at making friends.

But the older I get, the more I realize that they were right. We have a zillion acquaintances but few authentic friends . . . those people that will drive you to the airport at five in the morning . . . or help you move into that nine-story walk-up you love so much. These are the people that make up your own cast of Friends. All the others are extras.

That's why writing this chapter is fucking hard for me because I'm about to offend the only people who would drive me to the airport . . . or help me move. Many of these people have been there for me in some tight spots. Some have listened to me during my darkest days. And they have listened well. They may not have always had the best advice, or any advice at all. But they were willing to be there and love—mostly, unconditionally.

The conditions tended to kick in when I was willing to talk about my biggest secret of all. The gay thing. At first, they promise nothing will ever change. "Thank you so much for trusting me enough to share this secret with me. You know I'll always love you no matter what. I will always be there for you. I will always be praying for you."

They will pray for you until they realize their prayers are not being answered in the way they expected—no matter how many times they've asked God to intervene and make me straight. They get so damn frustrated when I keep on "choosing to be gay."

Even as I'm writing these words, it has occurred to me that it's this damn gay thing that puts the conditions back into unconditional love. Many of us have been told that Jesus loves everyone. He came to earth to die for even the most horrible person's sins. Hitler could be forgiven if he had only thought to ask. Jeffrey Dahmer, the sick cannibalistic bastard from my home state who liked to drill holes into teenage Vietnamese kids, then pop their bodies in his freezer—somehow came to know Jesus before he was murdered in prison. Even he was forgiven.

And will probably be eating at the great feast. Maybe no Vietnamese food—but he will be there dining with the best of them. And if God has the sense of humor I trust that he has—or at least the sense to seat in alphabetical order—Dahmer's place card will be right smack in between Paul Crouch and Jerrry Falwell.

(If they even get invited—or maybe *that* will be hell for them.)

So, mass murderers, tax cheats, gluttons, divorcees, child molesters, fornicators, fivenacators and those that make illegal U-turns will all be forgiven. If only they ask. And it's only if they stay on the straight and narrow.

The gift of unconditional love wrapped in grace does not apply for those damned, despicable gays.

I find it interesting how our big mega-church system has created some interesting loopholes for sin and certain sinners. Jesus, when he walked the earth never once mentioned the gay thing. Even though it's pretty much all we hear from the media owned by Foxes and those claiming to be Religious and Right. It seems it didn't even make Jesus's top ten of the sins that pissed him off.

Pride really seemed to get his goat. As well as choosing to ignore the poor in favor of buying yet another expensive luxury boat.

Even though he talked often about the sanctity of marriage—and how by divorcing your spouse you basically turn him or her into a whore—the new mega-church system has found that little rule to be an absolute bore. In our new world order Jesus can coyly look the other way when an unhappily married couple decides to break their marriage covenant and conveniently part ways.

If the divorced couple happens to attend a Christian church, they may be asked to step down from their leadership position for a few months, until the ugliness settles and then the new improved individuals can work their way back up the leadership ladder . . . starting first as lowly greeters and ending up once again as celebrated worship leaders. As long as you are generous every week the church will promise to turn the other cheek.

Blessed Family Tithes

(A church family that pays together stays together—no matter what.)

But those rules only apply to acceptable sinners with acceptable sins. The homos have their own private hell to contend with. And the best part is they don't have to die first. They get to live it right here on earth . . . over and over again . . . often at the hands of some of their closest of friends.

A few years ago, when my first book *God.com* was about to hit the shelves, I flew back home to take my Mom and stepfather to a beautiful bed-and-breakfast and spend an amazingly honest weekend with them. I decided that since my book was going to reveal that I happened to prefer the company of men, it was only fair that they hear it directly from me rather than read it on the page, or worse yet—hear it second hand from one of their two friends.

At first things were going swimmingly. I struggled to get the words out and when they finally came they seemed to be met with a modicum of compassion and understanding. There was even a little laughter.

At first.

But something happened when they had a chance to sleep on my little revelation. The next day was filled with awkward silences and the inability to hold each others' gaze—much less a conversation.

I found that the best that they could do was look the other way, and that has pretty much been the rule since then. Even though I was willing to be honest with them and the world at large, they decided that even talking about this subject ever again was way too fucking hard.

And so we didn't.

And if the subject ever came up—and it rarely ever did—I was reminded that it was simply a choice. Decide not to sin. Just like they did.

I believe that not everyone is necessarily 100 percent straight or 100 percent gay. There is probably this vague little continuum where we all fall somewhere in between. Yes, I've met guys who seem to retch and vomit at the thought of being with another man. But I've also been with some of those die-hard breeders who after throwing back a few beers were no longer *die* . . . only *hard* and the events that unfolded were definitely queer. The lines begin to blur and fade and those who have only walked the straight and narrow may end up straight but not quite so narrow.

This sexual preference thing isn't all black and white. But I know this for a fact: for most, it isn't a choice. I am happy for those who have the option because quite honestly there is probably no more difficult path to take than that of being gay. Why would anyone in their right mind make this choice? Growing up you are teased mercilessly, thrown into lockers and locked into stalls and they call you a faggot before you even know what that means. Then, after a lifetime of fighting your merciless peers, you fight yourself for years and years trying to prove them all wrong—even though down deep you know that those mean little bastards were quite right.

(And yet, so wrong.)

Then for those who have faith in an all-loving and benevolent Creator, there is the hellish war that ensues where the *sick* gay son or daughter must continually put themselves in the balance between heaven and hell while they work overtime to make themselves "well." Sermon after sermon and images of "loving Christians" with hateful and vitriolic signs of the times are broadcast over and over on the news—all continually confirming that God Hates Fags. Period. And there is nothing you can do.

(Oh, yeah—you can choose.)

Exodus International and other X-gay ministries have offered thousands false hope that they can be changed—that they can be straight. They have classes for lesbians on how to apply make-up and they teach those boys who are a little light in the loafers to learn to walk without a swish—to learn to walk like a man and talk without a lisp.

> (So now what do we do with a pig in lipstick . . .
> and a puss in boots?)

They help with outside appearances. But what they don't understand is that their well-meaning but dangerous interferences are creating profound conflicts on the inside—contributing to an excessively high rate of gay youth suicide.

An A.D.D Reality—Unhappy and Gay

According to current research out of
Denmark, gay youth are four times more
likely to attempt suicide than those who are
straight. And shockingly—in the past two
weeks, 4 teens in the U.S. decided it was too
difficult to be gay and continue to live. One
loving 13-year old shot himself in the head,
and a talented young violinist jumped off the
George Washington Bridge.*

I won't even begin to speculate on how many well-intentioned
Christians have pushed a young struggling gay person to the verge
of suicide or worse. I know for a fact that the thought had crossed
my mind . . . time and time again.

A lesbian pastor friend in Laguna Beach used to get all teary-eyed
every time she would teach on the subject—because she said she
had personally lost so many friends who had been thrown to the
pits of depression by well-meaning men—

Who insisted that to find God's love there is something first that
they would have to do—be straight. Yet when asked how? They
had absolutely no clue.

Trust Jesus. Pray more.
                Fast.
                Pray faster.

---

* Qin P, Agerbo E, Mortensen PB (2003). Suicide risk in relation to socioeco-
nomic, demographic, psychiatric, and familial factors: a national register-based
study of all suicides in Denmark, 1981-1997. American Journal of Psychiatry,
160(4): 765-72.

I can't think of anything fucking harder than to make the choice to be gay. Although it has become a lot easier for us in this more enlightened age, the headlines continue to prove that there is still so much rage aimed at anyone and everything that can be labeled gay.

My dear friend who had been waiting in the closet until the tender age of 62 . . . said that when he was young and hot, being gay was something you could not do.

And live to tell about it.

So he gave up any thought about living honestly and free on the outside of his little hell, and instead he chose to marry a woman and father children and provide well . . . so those kids could have a life that was a whole lot better than his. So that they could have a life filled with love, and maybe he'd even have some gay kids who would have the opportunity to live unlike him—open, honest and free.

An A.D.D. Travesty

Ironically, his teenaged grandson finally had to leave his Christian school after being called a fag, over and over by a majority of his classmates. He couldn't face the day knowing that the faculty would do nothing to keep the bullying at bay. They looked the other way—suggesting this brilliant boy continue to pray that God would make him straight, or at the very least that he would help him act less gay. Thank God we live in this enlightened age.

So it has been hard for people like him, and people like me—when we have to witness the self-righteous sinners who don't struggle with being gay—(yet they struggle with other things,) as they tell us over and over that if God is truly powerful, if God is really God then why don't we have enough faith to allow him to set us free.

And they are giving us this mouthful, while they over-eat, or are coveting a brand new kitchen or lavish addition to their large house, while they pass the homeless man and look the other way—gossiping about their neighbor . . . who happens to be gay.
Yeah. It is fucking hard, to be judged.

And it's even harder to choose to love.

And sometimes harder still, to choose to be loved.

But that is our only choice, if we want to walk in the footsteps of the One who gave his very life . . .

For sinners like you, and sinners like me—and anyone else who is foolish enough to believe.

Even the fools who make it *so* fucking hard to believe.

6.
Growing
through the
Motions.

Doing Yoga while in heat.

Eons ago I began a journey with God—a wild spiritual ride that began with a simple request I penned in my journal. I wrote: "I would
love for God to speak to me." Although I don't know much, I do
know this. If you want something from God, all you have to do is
ask. And if that something is the thing he also wants . . . you are
certain to receive it. As it turns out, it seems God isn't so much
about luxury cars and winning the lottery, no matter what those
Mega-Pastors may lead you to believe. He seems to be a tad less
materialistically minded and more into the zen kinds of requests.
Like learning how to turn distractions off and hear him speak
through the silence . . . like learning how to forgive and return
good for evil, and turning other cheeks.

God did in fact begin to speak to me—and that happened when
I took some time to turn things off. Like the radio, newspapers,
films and magazines. When I carved out a good solid two weeks

of silence—God began to speak. And man was he chatty. I guess he doesn't have as many friends as he used to—

It's a pity, as he turned out to be the best friend I've ever had.

I miss him.

Unfortunately I seem to have turned everything back on—and more. Distraction is so much more readily available than drugs. And cheaper too! But the results are nearly the same. Days go by and nothing is accomplished. The soul becomes threadbare and it is nearly impossible to love anyone.

Especially yourself. And Jesus said love your brother like you love yourself . . .

You do the math.

But the good news is, true friends never ever abandon you. Even when you behave like a selfish twitching addict waiting around for the next adrenaline fix.

God is standing by, waiting for you to knock on his door and merely say, "Hi."

So after writing that first book, the letters poured in from people all over the world. People who suddenly didn't feel alone anymore because I shared some of my personal struggles with them, and I shared a glimmer of Hope—hope that God really does love them, love me. Even with all our shit.

The point is: don't quit.

The problem that generally arises after you write something that has a shred of value is that the people reading like to make you a hero. They seem to forget that the stories that they have read are stories of brokenness, heartache, fragility and all the other disgusting stuff that makes us so painfully human. They minimize your stories of how God turns your poop into potpourri—and instead they elevate you to the position of Pope. At least the Pope of pop Christian prose.

(And there is NO shortage of gray smoke being blown up your robe.)

So one of those guys was someone who lived in the back woods of West Virginia. He was a youth pastor in a small town struggling to bring hope to kids ravished by abandonment, abuse, rejection and neglect . . . all while he battled those same scary demons that had been plaguing him for as long as he could remember. Mostly because he was gay.

He tried everything he could to fix it. He even married a great girl and decided to choose the straight and narrow and hope that time and heterosexual sex would erase the longing he had to be in the arms of another man.

Which only led him into the arms of another married man . . . who was doing the same thing . . . while hiding behind a ministry of his own.

Connor wrote me letters asking for help. He tried on several occasions to have us meet so we could talk face to face. I think he imagined that I held the keys to the Kingdom . . . when in truth, I didn't even know where the Kingdom was . . . exactly.

I never did meet him. Or even speak to him on the phone in the period where I thought I may have had things figured out and answers to his questions. Instead, we met years later when I had no real good advice. Nothing at all, only friendship to offer.

He admired the freedom I had found in my own personal journey. He envied the way I lived openly with my Christian friends, while he hid behind his marriage vows, hoping beyond hope that God would somehow find it in his heart to forgive him for the lie he was living while trying to find the truth.

Over the course of our friendship I have fielded a number of his letters where he wrote how he wished he could die, so the madness would be over and he could finally rest. On one occasion he thought he would offer his heart for a transplant, but I had to remind him that the medical community doesn't generally accept hearts from healthy, young *living* donors. This gay thing is fucking hard—for so many, in so many different ways. And no matter which path you choose to take—there are some days you think you can't go on.

After spending time together recently he wrote me a letter where he expressed just that.

James,

This will be an e-mail i will regret, but after watching Hairspray and some hallmark movie i find myself once again having a moist center and not the normal small cock and balls.

i want to thank you. why?

Mainly, just for being you. I will admit that you are a different James than I imagined for the past several years. that is not a bad thing. Thank you for letting me in. you didn't have to, but you did.

You have been a person i have admired for years. You were my hero . . . but now you are no longer my hero. Heroes never truly connect with the ones they are saving and they never let anyone know who they really are. They stay carefully hidden behind their mask.

I listen to the Keane song you played for me—once in awhile—the one that asks if it's a waste of time trying to be friends.

I know it isn't a waste, but is it worth me reaching out when we live miles apart—even if we lived nearby i don't fit in with your crowd, i am more than likely going to deny who I am, and most days I don't even know if I can take the craziness anymore. I'm surrounded by people, yet I feel so alone. Some days I just think it would be easier for everyone if I were just—no more.

I don't know what is going to happen down the road. I don't know how big of a role you will play in my life, you have added a few more questions to my journey . . . it turns out i needed them. Thank you for taking off your mask and choosing instead to be my friend.

Connor

Connor caught me on a rare, soft morning, so I sent him this response, a response I wanted to share with you because you may be struggling too . . . with questions and doubts and maybe even thoughts that it may just be a little bit easier after that bottle of OxyContin and a bourbon chaser or two . . .

Connor-

Diesel and a friend are in bed fast asleep . . .

I just came down for a clove and a 9-shot iced latte. My head is spinning from the smoke and the cool, bittersweet taste of the almost burnt Italian roast coffee . . .

My mind is full of random thoughts . . . thoughts like, "why did I leave the love of my life and now I have a gorgeous friend upstairs sleeping peacefully with my Pit Bull?"

I have made so many mistakes since I left L.A.

I know that I often make God weep in his gin and tonic for all the selfish, ridiculous things I do . . . repeatedly.

I guess I am writing this to let you know that you are not alone when you look at your life and the things you have done or the things you do that you don't like . . . or that you may feel are a massive contradiction.

I started doing hot yoga for the wrong reasons. One of those reasons is sleeping with Diesel right now.

But it's funny how God works.

The yoga is the hardest thing I have done in a long, long time. It is the most physically torturous thing I have put myself through—and as a result I am learning that I need more discipline in my life. Yoga has also begun to focus my mind (I think the little banana juggling chimps who live in my head are beginning to die from heat exhaustion when I'm in that damn room doing impossible things for 90 minutes.)

And that new clarity is helping me see where I make the same poor choices over and over. (Like having Nachos and Long Island's the night before Yoga for instance.)

I'm also learning about grace.

But the greatest thing I've learned in Hot Yoga doesn't have anything to do with poses . . . it's that last 8 minutes when the yoga nazi tells you to lie flat on your mat. They turn the heat down and the ceiling fans on. They pass out chilled moist towels that have been scented with lavender and you just lie there with every part of your body completely exhausted and you get lost in the crazy Buddhist gongs and chimes and the heady buzz of the endorphins that are surging through your body—and it is all because you didn't quit early . . . you didn't give up . . . There is no greater feeling on earth.

You are very hard on yourself, Connor.

And you are human making mistakes all the time. Just like me.

But this is only one 90 minute class.

We are at the 30 minute point or so . . . and the heat is really hot.

But one day we will lie flat . . . with the ceiling fans on and the cool, lavender-scented towels on our faces and the chimes and gongs will be replaced with harps and some awful Contemporary Christian singer's voice . . .

And we will feel so good that we pushed through.

We endured.

And that is when we enter the Rest.

Yeah. I'm not the guy you imagined. And you're not the guy I imagined.

But imagine this . . .

We are friends . . .

Obviously the juggling chimps have recovered from the heat.

And there are more bananas in the air than I'd like to admit.

Your light shines brightly, my friend.

And I am warmed.

Have a very Merry Christmas.

(And whatever you do—just don't quit—I can't do this alone)

James

After sending this letter I felt so alive again. It felt so good to be writing and I could feel the tangible love of God fill the room. I suddenly realized that the letter I had written to Connor was a letter I needed to share with you . . . and the dozens of other Connors who were wrestling with the same questions, the same fears, messy attractions, affairs and self-loathing. And then I realized the letter was for me.

So I carried my laptop to the third floor where my dog and my beautiful friend were sleeping, and I asked if I could read the letter I had written. After listening to the whole thing, my sweet, gorgeous friend looked up at me with warm and sleepy eyes and asked, "So I don't get it, is Connor taking yoga now too?"

Ohhhmm . . . No you didn't!!

I closed my computer and realized it was probably time to shut things off again for a while and get rid of all my distractions—young, beautiful and otherwise—and say, "Hi" to my very best friend.

The conversations were always richer. There were fewer misunderstandings. And he knows me better than I even know myself . . .

Yeah.
It's time.

7.
Sin Tax.

The **wages** of sin are death.*
(Prices do not include tax, licensing and dealer destination charges)

Sin. A pretty big scary-ass kind of word. And for the most part it's a word that is used only by over-coiffed TV evangelists and manic street preachers—two common characters populating the landscape of the "Surreal World."

Years ago, Madonna may have occasionally mentioned the word sin, but when she did, a line usually formed. Tickets would go for more than 300 bucks, ripped black men with dreads stripped down nude and leashes and collars were applied. A healthy little game of truth or dare ensued, measurements and photos were taken, a coffee table book was published and everybody went home a winner. Maybe a little bit sore, but a winner nonetheless.

Like a Virgin.

With a twist.

Today, however—the word sin is back to its old scary self. It's usually used to condemn someone who does something worse than you do—making you feel oh-so-much better about yourself. In fact, the word sin is usually all you need to send someone straight to hell. Most of us don't like the word, and we tend to avoid it

---

*Romans 6:23

when possible. That's probably why most of us gays avoid going to church—because that is the place where the word is used most—and in terms of sinners, homos are the worst.

In the Bible, there are so many sins that it's nearly impossible to keep track. And though sinful same-sex antics are only mentioned a handful of times—for some reason the church today always circles back. Reminding us over and over about the dangers of doing crack(s).

Hey, if the Bible is correct and the wages of sin really are death, then I guess logic says I'm going to die anyway. I may as well get paid for my antics and have a hell of a good time on my way down. I may even get to kiss Madonna. Or at the very least, watch her kiss Britney. (Back when that was cool.)

And speaking of same-sex kisses . . . how in the world did this gay thing become such a flash point between Christians and fags anyway?

An A.D.D. Divinity

In all the passages of the Bible that quote
Jesus while he was here—he never once
mentioned homosexuality. Now doesn't that
seem a tad bit queer? Was he simply
distracted by a bad case of A.D.D?

I know both sides carry some of the blame—gay pride is not always expressed in ways that spotlight our greatest contributions to society. And often those large contributions are being waved at society covered only in a thong, or less. But as crass as that may seem to a Puritan watching their 52" flickering flat screen, nothing could be more offensive, nothing more obscene, than those God-fearing idiots who rush out to where they can best be seen, parading around in their prideful self-righteousness, waving American flags and hand-made signs reminding us all that

God
Hates Fags!

Or,

G.A.Y.
(Got AIDS Yet?)

And of course the always popular and ever-clever

Turn or Burn.

I bet God cries every time he sees those God-damned signs where his name is used in vain. I bet his heart aches every time he sees hateful words hurled from a self-proclaimed religious right-hand man—carrying out "The Lord's work," targeting the very people that God loves passionately, insanely, jealously. I'm convinced that these fags, homos and dykes are some of God's favorite kids. And this dangerous band of hate-mongers have effectively done their job at convincing "the family" that they are no longer wanted at home.

And so we are
forced to roam.

(Roaming charges do apply. See service provider's very fine print.)

Anne Lamott, one of my favorite authors, sort of reframed the whole idea of sin and the punishment that comes from sin for me. She said that often we are not punished for the sin, so much as we are punished by *the sin.*

An A.D.D. Moment

The Greek word for sin is Hamartano—which means "to miss the mark." And when we miss the mark—we are no longer in the zone—and we suffer by not having the perfect. We now live in the imperfect and that isn't as comfortable. In some instances we miss the mark so much that we wander in front of an oncoming bus, or a deadly disease. These, to me, are not God's judgment and wrath—they're simple cause-and-effect relationships. You step off a building and gravity kicks in, not God's temper. The wages of missing the mark in this case will vary based on the span from rooftop to asphalt. In some cases the price is a neck brace, in others a casket. In either case the wages of sin are not God's fault—they are asphalt. So if you happen to miss the perfect path, you may suffer . . . and in some cases your suffering may be some dumb asphalt!

XXX-mas

Years ago, when I was a tortured soul who didn't like gay things or gay people (or my gay self, for that matter) I ended up spending Christmas in San Francisco with a friend from graduate school. He was even more confused about his sexuality than me. And at the time, that was hard for anyone to believe. He was a Jesuit priest who has struggled wildly as he tried to juggle his faith and his sexuality. His life had been one big paradoxical roller coaster ride. One minute he was dressed in black spandex and dancing at Rage, and the next time I would see him he was in all black apart from the collar which was white—and he had signed a contract of chastity, poverty and stupidity. (Now wait, I don't think I have that right). I have nothing but love for my friend and I have ridden my share of roller coasters in my attempt to figure this out. But thank God I haven't signed any binding contracts to keep my pants buttoned tight.

So there we were, two wildly confused boys, on the night before Christmas in Martooni's, a little gay piano bar near the Castro.

I was thinking that this was my most ironic and unorthodox Christmas eve to date, all the while we sipped apple martinis and sang along with the Christmas carols. Old men in sweaters pushed their way to the piano to belt out the words of the well-worn holiday faves.

But something happened in that dimly lit place with all those men donning their gay apparel and singing a tiresome litany of inane little songs. A young guy with kind eyes made his way to the microphone at the piano and from somewhere deep inside his impassioned soul, the most heartbreaking version of "O Holy Night" came pouring out into that bar filled with singing sodomites.

"O Holy night, the stars are brightly shining, it is the night of my dear savior's birth."

The crowd of misunderstood men knew every single word of that most beautiful tribute to the man who couldn't be more misunderstood by both the religious right and the immoral majority.

Maybe it was because it was Christmas and the clean white snow tends to cover up all the shit that we have trudged through the rest of the year—helping us forgive the confederacy of dunces that so often surround us. Or maybe it was because somewhere, deep inside, this gathering of his sons and daughters knew the truth. The Jesus as seen on TV is not the real Jesus. The real Jesus loves the broken, the battered, the weary, the lonely, the unlovable and unloved. And he especially loves those damned sinners who can never seem to get it right. Because he is the only one who can help us get it right. And getting it right may look different for you than it does for me.

God showed up that night in the little gay piano bar in the Castro. I could feel him there as his tears poured down my cheeks. I now saw those broken-down men (the very men I hadn't much liked before) with God's love-soaked eyes. In an instant, I realized that these were his special boys. Those who had been rejected and misunderstood from the day they were born, or maybe even before. These were the ones that he came to love and he wasn't going to give up and he wasn't going to let go—come hell or high water. His love was and is unconditional and I knew at that moment that it was time for someone to let these, his lost boys know . . . that they may have been rejecting the wrong Jesus, the Jesus they assumed had rejected them first. And after a fucking long hard life of painful rejection these kids learned how to avoid the pain by launching a counter-attack faster than the Bush family can take us all to war.

Bush Whacked

In that moment, I realized that Jesus didn't reject them at all. And that meant he didn't reject me—at all. Instead, he dropped his Creator credit and Executive Producer title to play the lead in a passion play. He robed himself in sweating, stinking, pooping human flesh—to show us how this works. Wars have been waged through the ages over our misunderstandings of God—and so Jesus decided to walk it out and show us what it means to love, serve and give . . . to the very last drop.

Unconditional love . . . for those of us who have missed the mark, those who have lost their way. Road weary sinners like us who will go on sinning until our dying day.

No gimmicks.
No strings.
Just love and hope and promise . . .

As the gay men's chorale continues to sing . . .

> **"Long lay the world in sin and error pining,**
> **'til he appears and the soul felt its worth."**

Sin.

It isn't such a big scary word after all. As I mentioned before, if you look it up in the Greek language you find out that it simply means, "missing the mark." A "sinner" is one who missed the mark. One who may have lost the way. I miss the mark every single day. I will until I take my last breath. And so in that place I have to rest . . . because it says over and over in the Bible that Jesus came for sinners . . . those who have missed the mark. And so I guess I'm in the bonus round, because I have proof that he came for fuck-ups just like me.

My only job in this whole crazy journey is to look past my demons and choose to believe. Jesus said he would take care of the rest. I can only rest.

And trust.
I've tried my whole life to fix my shit. And guess what. I'm not fixed. But Jesus never told people to get fixed up, cleaned up and dressed up then come to him. He said, come to me all you who are tired, sick, desperate and carrying the weight of the world on your shoulders and I will give you rest. That is good news for sinners like you and sinners like me. And the word Gospel means "Good news."

And this good news is good enough for me.

God picks the strangest places to make appearances—that first Christmas eve it was in a small, stinky-ass barn—literally on the backside of bumfuck Egypt and this particular Christmas eve it was in a gay piano bar called Martoonis in the Castro—the heart of our modern day Sodom and Gomorrah.

I have never felt so much love for strangers as I did that night in San Francisco. And I knew that whether we were sinners or not—somehow in that place on Christmas eve we had all, for a brief moment in time, hit that mark—together.

O,
Holy Night.

8.
Touched

(Inappropriately)

by an Angel(o).

Llove—with an L of a difference.

I think down deep we may all secretly hope that the next time we fall in love it will be with an angel—that perfect person with a heart of gold. The one who will never hurt you, never desert you and will love you perfectly through all space and time. That soul mate who loves you with every fiber of his being. The one who will fight for you, die for you and ultimately live by your side until the end of time. No rejection, no betrayal and never a harsh word spoken. He wakes up smiling and his laughter is the elixir to heal all wounds. He speaks the language of love, loves to touch and be touched and will remind you throughout the day that you are a genius, an artist, a modern day prophet—a renaissance man.

Yeah—I would love to love an angel and be loved by one just the same. I think that maybe this little misguided fantasy explains the wild promiscuity in our culture. And when I say our culture, I mean gay and straight alike. We all want one version or another of an angel—that perfect missing piece that will bring you peace. The person to complete you, not compete with you. The one like no other—because he or she does not exist. So we fuck our way to that dead-end alley where we run smack into that big wall of bricks—and the jolt to our head helps us realize that we have had it all and yet we have nothing. No one person will ever fill that void or make us whole. And so it goes. And then in that place of understanding we can either settle for one of the fallen angels that we have come upon—or one that has come upon us.

Cum and go . . .

Or you leave town to fuck your way to the back of a new dead-end alley where you meet those same cold bricks with a different Zip. And depending on your level of intelligence or degree of insanity—you can continue this promiscuous cycle for years on end. Wash, rinse, repeat.

Begin again.
(Well, hello bricks—we meet again)

At some point it becomes clear that there is no singularly perfect mate that will make you complete. And that is not such a bad thing. Because I think the real goal is to become complete—and then find that fallen angel with whom you can work out the bugs and the kinks and become even more complete as a person and as a partner as you make your way down that selfless journey called love.

And love is a selfless journey if you want to do it right.

If we continue to try to have our needs met by the other—we will at some point burn them out. Ultimately they will have nothing left to give and our only option is to move on once again to find yet another giver from whom we can take everything until our cannibalistic hunger exceeds the resources available to feed our voracious need.

Wash, rinse
repeat.

Just two fleas, each hoping the other is a dog.

But I'm starting to learn that true love, authentic love, love that was intended by the Author of love—is a love that is all about giving. And forgiving. And maybe even allowing the object of our love and affection to pursue their dream even if that dream does not include "me."

Love is an act of selfless giving—giving that comes out of the center of who we are. Love wells up from somewhere deep inside, and the more we give from that place—the more we build our partner—the more we give him or her strength to pour out selflessly as well. My lifting you up does not diminish me—instead it gives you a stronger and higher footing from which to lift me higher, from which place I can reach back to you, to bring us both higher than we could have ever climbed on our own. Or using each other as steppingstones.

This is authentic love. A life of giving. True living.

Loving,
　　　learning,
　　　　　　nurturing,
　　　　　　　　　exploring,
　　　　　　　　　　　　slipping,
　　　　　　　　　　　　　　　falling then forgiving.

It is never easy but it is authentic and pure. And I think it is from this place of selfless surrender and reckless giving that we begin to experience life in the way that is truly worth living. A life that our God always intended.

So now that I've spelled out the secret of success in life and love and other heavenly pursuits—I am brought to that place of finding love in the first place.

You never know where love will find you. Or how it will find you. But inevitably it does find you. Even when you think you've found a clever hiding spot. But sometimes love comes in a package you may not recognize—like a formerly fallen Angel in a clever disguise (like a goofy Santa hat).

And the love you find may not be what you expected. It may be so much more.

I spotted my Angel years ago in the heart of the City of Angels while I was working in my dimly lit office on an un-inspired script—my heart wasn't in it and I was losing interest—when I heard the unmistakable laughter of a gay man across the hall in the copy room.

I waited for a moment looking surreptitiously through my open door waiting to see what sort of queer person dared to work at a Christian production company. It was a little like a Jew stoking the ovens of Auschwitz—hoping not to be discovered while doing his very best to fit in—to fuel the fires to keep his paycheck while doing as little damage as he possibly can to his brothers and sisters who would be fodder for his flamey flames.

Wow, that was way too fucking dramatic. I apologize.

A few moments later Angelo Idoll—

(Yes, that's his real name—and if that wasn't enough he went by Angel—my God, this was quickly becoming my own private Rent.)

—came flying out of that little copy room wearing a dorky Santa hat with a great big boingy spring that made the fluffy ball at the top of his hat bobble and swing. I was swept into the heavenly blue in his crystalline eyes, the eternal smile—and angelic radiance that couldn't be duplicated, not even in the copy room.

Smitten. Touched by an Angel(o) . . . a shiny new Idoll with an additional L—that's an L of a difference and I knew in an instant that I could love this boy well.

But the problem with this perfect little double L'ed idol was that he came with one L of a twist. The formerly fallen Angel had years before led a gay life—but decided to pursue the straight and narrow and found himself a wife. I figured he was one of those that Exodus deceived, a "Ho Mo, No Mo." I was devastated—but exquisitely intrigued.

The short version of the story is this. We became friends—the three of us—Angel and his amazing wife Amanda. We spent a lot of time together, cooking, shopping and talking about being gay, being X-gay and what that means. Until meeting the Idolls I had pretty much written off the Exodus types—those who so wanted to please God that they were willing to deceive themselves (and those they tried to convert) while they crawled back into an even more stifling closet—because now that closet held a wife!

My problem with that whole scenario is that they seemed as gay as ever . . . burning down the house. And I could not forgive them. They were doing more damage than good as far as I was concerned, because I'd believed for so long that God would change me if I only jumped through enough hoops. If I fasted, prayed and believed long enough, this whole nightmare would be over and we could move on into a simpler chapter of life. And since this never seemed to happen for me, I felt I was doing something wrong—which always led to many shameful, sleepless nights.

But suddenly I am face to face with an authentic Angel. Or an Angelo, at least—(hey this was Southern California) and his fun-loving wife—and neither were spewing rhetoric or X-gay propaganda. They were being honest about their journey and their willingness to trust beyond what they could see.

But from time to time, my devilish little friend would set my imagination on fire with vivid descriptions of his "old life of sin"—with his legs in the air or talk of the boys he would pin. And just as my imagination would burst into unquenchable flames, this beguiling little Idoll would then tell me how much his life had changed. Now that he had found the love of his life. And as much as I wanted that to be me, that person happened to be his wife.

Angel became painfully honest with me, especially when Amanda wasn't around. He mentioned over and over how his temptation had not ended. Sometimes it felt that it was slightly suspended—but often, the straight path was only possible through a disciplined act of his will. And though he enjoyed having sex with a woman, sometimes it wasn't enough, and avoiding extra-curricular romps with hot boys was becoming tough. And in the case of our friendship, he admitted freely to his feelings for me and at the same time he set some boundaries in place—so that we could navigate a friendship where neither of us would lose face.

Or sleep.

For a time that worked. But I learned quickly that loving an Angel was harder than hell—especially an Angel Idoll with a Goddamned extra L.

Touched (inappropriately) by an Angel(o).

Finally one drunken night, after a satisfying party had wrapped up at my house, the three of us piled into my bed to watch a movie on my giant screen. It was when his wife fell asleep between us that Angel did something not so angelic—and it was something his sleeping wife would wake to see, undoubtedly confirming her deepest fear that her little converted husband Angel was still completely queer.

An A.D.D. Aside

Did you realize that the original founders of
Exodus International have gone back to their
old ways—even though this same
organization promises gays all over the world
that with enough concentration, prayer and
fasting—they too can be changed?* And this
just in—John Smid, former director of Love in
Action, the nation's oldest and largest X-gay
ministry, admitted on his blog, "I've never
met a man who experienced a change from
homosexual to heterosexual." And what's
more, he is now making public apologies for
inflicting so much pain.**

Now—what to do with this. Your imagination may be running
wild, but his indiscretion was ridiculously tame. Tame to me, but
apparently not to an angry wife. This little advance would completely rock their newly married life.

It would be disingenuous to pretend that this was an easy pill to
swallow. In my first three attempts at writing this chapter, I nailed
my little angel to a tree. And I showed him absolutely no mercy.
Once again I had found myself caught up in the fantasy that maybe
I, too, can be straight, if I jump through the right hoops and have
the tenacity to wait. While working on the *700 Club*, almost every
featured artist formerly known as gay would share on camera how
God had made them straight—the studio audience would clap politely, the segment ended nicely and the lights would dim and the
network would go to a break. And like clockwork, they would exit
stage left and immediately head my way.

---

*(From the article, "Turning Off Gays" on Salon.com, July 18, 2005,
http://www.salon.com/2005/07/18/ungay/).

**John Smid's blog, Grace Rivers: http://www.gracerivers.com/gays-repent/

"Hey big guy, would you like to grab dinner or maybe some drinks?" They'd ask with an unbelievable straight face. And once again, my hopeful heart would sink.

"My God, that sounds great, but what would your lesbian of a wife or 17 lovely children think?"

The truth is, no matter how much this sort of double standard angered me, I realize now that no matter what path any of us choose to take, from time to time, we will all fall into hypocrisy. I battle it all the time in my own way—so why should I harshly judge another frail human if they also lose their way? (Even if it is a way that I believe may bring more harm than good.)

(I don't want to come off sounding like a bitter queen—that is so not a good look for me.)

As much as I wanted to use this incident to point out the ridiculous sham these two misguided Idolls were living, I suddenly realized what the nagging extra L in Idoll was actually for. This is the L of true Love—authentic love where you L-evate the other above your immediate perceived needs and you place them in the place of safety where they can achieve their dream.

Not yours.

I suddenly realized that as much as I would love to make love to this Angel—to take him home and call him my own—this gorgeous little Idoll had a dream that was uniquely his, and that dream involved a home. A home that he had already created with a partner of his choosing and although his eye may stray from time to time and I may fall in his field of vision, he had already made his decision—to pursue the straight and narrow, no matter what he may be feeling. This was a decision that was uniquely his and required no defense. And if we are truly going to celebrate diversity, then we must allow everyone on earth—especially our friends—to pursue their path no matter what that path may be or how ridiculous it seems. It is their own dream. And maybe, God's own dream.

Before I was touched inappropriately, Angel had pointed out a blog written by the president of Exodus International where he speaks of obedience over orientation. How orientation—gay or straight—may be firmly in place, but when God calls us to a life of obedience, sacrifice, celibacy, or marriage with a specific gender, it is far more important to pursue obedience rather than satisfy our most basic needs. And in that place of obedience, God is truly pleased. After reading through the blog, I started thinking about my life and my own experiences with God. My path looks so much different than anyone I know but the bottom line is he wants me to trust him no matter what anyone else may think. And every time he has asked me for something, or made a promise, I have chosen to recklessly believe. Even if that meant moving 10,000 miles away. What I can honestly tell you is that in every single instance, no matter how outlandish the promise—he has been good for his word. Every single time.

Up until now, he has never promised to make me straight—so I guess I will go on recklessly believing while being completely gay.

The farther along I get on this journey, the more I am seeing that God isn't a God of black and white. What he expects of you is not necessarily what he expects of me—and I'm not to judge just because I don't agree. After living through this whole ridiculous mishap with my little double-L'ed Idoll, I decided to try my best to never judge an Angel—enlightened, misguided or otherwise inclined—and instead I would honor their journey as I hoped they would honor mine.

Hey Angel-

I have a thousand thoughts streaming through my mind right now. But I do believe the bottom line is this:

I may not agree with how you've chosen to
live. But your choice has nothing to do with
me. It has everything to do with what you
believe to be obedience to your God.

You and I are not all that different. And I
don't say that to be diplomatic.

There will be many well-meaning Christians
who will judge me for writing and publishing
Gay Conversations With God. They will know
in their heart of hearts that I have lost my
way—and that I'm leading others down a dark
and dangerous path. They will even be waiting with bated breath for me to encounter
God's fiery wrath.

And the supreme irony is that like you, I
believe that God is calling me to a life of
obedience above all things. And that level
of obedience keeps changing over time. For
right now, I think I am supposed to write
and publish an outrageous book telling of
God's love. For all of his children. All
types, all kinds. Even though the price
seems to be quite high. (I'm going to lose
my job—and maybe even the newfound love of
my mother. But hell, I know it's more important that I reach out to help my brother.)

As I continue on this messy journey I am
finding that God sometimes asks us to do extremely crazy things.

Like Isaiah, for instance.

God asked him to parade around *nude* for
three years. Did I mention—*nude*. Three thousand years before Showtime or HBO—

—to make a point.

(Global warming would have come in handy
back then—both for comfort and for appearance's sake)

Then there was Jeremiah, whom God told
2xist™ for months in only his Calvins–and
originally he was supposed to cook his meals
on fires of human poopLogs!™

So . . .

I am at an interesting crossroads.

Moving forward scares the shit out of me.
Standing still exhausts me. And I know I
have to be obedient, no matter how much
judgment and wrath will come my way.

In my morning reading yesterday I found this
in an old book my mom gave me years ago:

"When God, by his Spirit through his Word
gives you a clear vision of his will, you
must "walk in the light" of that vision . . .
if you don't walk in the light of that you
will sink to a level of bondage never envi-
sioned by our Lord. Mentally disobeying the
"heavenly vision" will make you a slave to
ideas and views that are completely foreign
to Jesus Christ. Don't look at someone else
and say, "Well, if he can have those views
and prosper than why can't I? You have to
walk in light of the vision that has been
given to you. Don't compare yourself with
others and judge them–that is between God
and them."

There are times I look at you and your life
and I'm envious. I would love to have what
you have. It is so simple. *Yeah, right*–but
you make it look that way.

Then, there are times I would love for you
to join me. To be my partner in crime–helping spread this outrageous message of love.

And then there are the rare times that I'm
angered by it all and I want to dismiss what

you have done and write it off as youthful
naiveté that will one day bite you in the
ass.

In my deepest heart of hearts I know it
isn't naiveté at all but obedience to the
heavenly vision God has given you.

The bottom line is this:

We must be faithful to the vision God has
given *us*–whatever that happens to be–no matter how crazy it may seem. Like a 90-year-
old believing he could pop a boner and usher
in the vast tribe of God's chosen people–
3400 years B.V. (before Viagra).

Or believing that a young teen girl was im-
pregnated by God himself.

Or, to be the husband of that young teen
girl and believe–even for a moment–that you
haven't hitched your ride to a lying little
whore.

And what's more . . .

The Bible is full of even more outrageous
stories that have become so routine, they
have lost their punch.
"Lying little whore" has become "Blessed
Virgin Mary."

But imagine the viscosity of the emotions
these real heroes of the faith had to be
wading through as they continued to believe
past what they could see.

And I believe that is where we are.

I am going to pursue the vision that God has
given me–a vision that is uniquely mine, and
I will honor the one he has given you.

And if I am completely wrong in any or all
of this, I believe it will be friends like
you who will help right my ship.

Thank you for your friendship.

James

Writing these words and living them out have proven to be more of a challenge than I ever imagined. Angelo and I, although we cared for each other, decided to disconnect completely while we allowed our deep emotional connection to subside—so that he could maintain a healthier relationship with his tender, formerly trusting wife.

And I honor that. For one thing I have learned—maybe the only thing I have learned—is that when you give God something sacrificially, he often gives that thing back. But this time that thing (whatever it may happen to be) is now much more healthy. And will be instrumental in helping you step into your heavenly vision, your dream. And although it would be a heavenly vision to spend the rest of this journey with an Angel Idoll by my side, I know that wouldn't be kosher with his lovely bride.

Angelo made a choice. He is taking a path that I don't feel called to take. As pissed off as I had become with his hypocrisy, and even the false hope that he may present to others like him—I realized down deep that I can still love him. And maybe with the more authentic L, I respect him enough to do what I can to help L-evate him, to give him a boost to help him find his path and live his dream. And I know that when our paths converge once again, he will be in an even stronger place. A place where he may L-evate me.

Yeah,
Llove sucks.

But if we live in it, authentically—we will become less judgmental of everyone we meet.

The homo, the harlot, the jew . . . the X-gay Angel and the Exodus crew.

Because it all boils down to this.

One day we will stand naked (and hopefully not ashamed) before a loving (not an angry) God and it's only going to be the two of us. Not another soul to blame for the things we have done, for the people we have mistreated and judged—or those who have done the same.

And once we finish up that face to face meeting with the God of the Universe and Creator of all, I am sure there will be time to get one of the millions of other angels to fall . . .

For me.

I mean, Christ. We have an eternity. Right!!??

Love without judgment and live without fear.
God is love.
And sometimes love is queer.
It may take a lifetime to figure out.

But maybe that's why we are here?

Postscript:
I'm still not planning on sending any monthly checks to those Exodus types. But I guess I need to respect them for doing what they think is right. I mean, I don't think God is crying in his gin and tonic over the Amish who think it honors God to live without electricity and use horses that can't take them far, but he is probably saying to himself . . . MohammaDammit—get a CAR!

9.

Jesus and his
Temple
Tantrum.

From everything I've read, Jesus seems like a chill guy. He comes off a little like Bono, but without the glasses. And maybe not the voice, I can't be sure. But I have a feeling he would have been a great musician had he put his heart into it. "Jesus, that sounds nice, but Christ, you have to practice more."

(Wait, that was *my* piano teacher.)

Rock star or not, Jesus drew huge crowds. And the reason was not because he did great stunts and talked real loud. (Although he wasn't above that). Mostly he moved quietly through crowds—and they followed. Because he said things that no one else was saying. Back in the day.

He said things that went against the grain.

Like, love your enemy. WTF?

Return good for evil. (That makes no sense.)

And when someone asks for your coat, give them your shirt too.

(Maybe even your pants?) Now that could be embarrassing depending on the setting, temperature and time of year.

And topping out the charts of today's least favorite of Jesus's teachings: "Give to absolutely anyone who asks . . . expecting nothing back." And that means you lose interest too.

Are we absolutely sure he was a Jew?

Whatever the case, the religious leaders of the day didn't like him. They had a system set up in place that kept them in power and this new kid on the block wasn't doing anything to help them.
In fact . . . his crazy teachings were going to run them out of business if the madness wasn't stopped.

Jesus threw a wrench in the system and sand in the machine. He kept suggesting that we sell all of our shit and give the proceeds to the poor. Or that we live in community and share what we have—giving and taking freely—according to our need.

Savior? You mean Red Menace!!

It was revolutionary. And we all know revolutionaries don't last long . . . because the people in power cannot remain in power if the masses sing along.

And they did, you know.

The crowds loved this Jesus. He was popular with young and old alike (like Bono) and he hung out with sinners and drinkers and whores . . . and I think he would have liked U2.

So the pious and pompous kept their eyes on him—they stuck to him like glue—to see what sort of crazy things they could nail him on—and I mean nail him on—because he was not a good law-abiding Jew.

In their eyes he was a miracle-working fool. A dangerous one. He kept breaking all their laws. It was becoming a bad habit—this healing on the Sabbath. And he always chose compassion over the law.

He basically made that the new law. The law of love.

And boy did he love.

Well.

He loved lepers and harlots, homos and blacks. It seemed that he was an equal opportunity savior. He gave freely to everyone and never seemed to expect anything back.

From all accounts he was an incredibly loving guy. He fed thousands, walked on water, forgave sinners and did a lot of healing (but he never slept on a Sealy—because he didn't have a home.)

God, this homeless man sure did ruffle some feathers and blow some minds. Even so, he had a lot of fans. Back in the day.

And he never lost his cool. Not even when the ship he was in was about to sink in a wind-whipped storm. Instead of working up a sweat, he crawled down into the hull and took a nap while keeping warm. When the nervous ship of fools woke him in sheer panic (their lack of faith bordering on Satanic) he laughed at their sea of doubt and told the waves where to go.

And they did.

Jesus was and is the master of paradox. In terms of the world's logic he was a crazy clown who had this uncanny way of turning the system upside down.

He said the most confusing things—like: Whoever loses his life, for Christ's sake, will find it. Yeah, right. He told us to give, and in giving, more would be given—back to us. Isn't that Karma? Oh God forbid. Isn't that what the Hindus did?

(WWHD? What would a Hindu do?)

My Karma
Ran Over
Your Dogma

He said follow me—but I can't see him—and he loved the unlovable with all of his heart. He especially loved the poor—he gave them life, sight forgiveness and wealth (no wait, that wealth part was someone else).

He gave freely of his time and his love, moving effortlessly through the social classes. He didn't start a mega church or officiate any masses. He was a respecter of no one and a lover of all—even kids. Especially kids. (Who are so damn loud on airplanes, yet so curious, cute and small).

> He is a ruler of angels but a servant of men. He
> loved every sinner and made hookers his friends.
> He moved through the people; he healed lepers
> and bleeders. He loves cross-dressers cross-
> bearers, homos and breeders.
> (From my book God.com.)

For all intents and purposes he loved most everybody well.

Well, except for the right and religious. He gave those guys hell!

It seems so interesting to me that if you read through the Bible, you find Jesus loving and forgiving everyone for almost everything.

Everything except being proud, pious and religious. That really got under his skin.

The one account of where he lost his mind came when he walked into the temple and felt covered in pious and prideful capitalistic slime.

God's house was meant to be a house of prayer—and everything but was going on there. They were buying and selling and doing all sorts of machinations to get the crowds to send their love gifts and monthly donations. They broadcast their pleas for money day and night! They held Big*Tent*Revivals™ and told the gullible masses that if they would give using plastic, they could be rich overnight . . .

(How fantastic!)

. . . or even debt free*

(*Current APR interest charges will be applied to your miracle.
If your payments are late or you are lacking in faith
we apply the default rate. Hell yeah, heaven can wait.)

Well, Jesus wasn't having any of it. He completely lost it and began screaming and shouting and flipping tables while he flipped his shit. He wasn't pleased with this sort of abomination and I don't think we've seen anything yet.

Throughout the Bible there is account after account of what sort of hell awaits those who fleece the flock. And if you've watched any Christian TV—you know we've all been flocked. Hard.

And those pious preachers with purple hair and promises to send you trinkets for all the cash you have to spare . . .

Will one day face the wrath they've been telling us about, every day right on the air. And truth be told, I don't believe they'll be spared.

But that's me. I'm not a fan. And neither was Jesus. He called the religious pretty crazy names like white-washed graves—stinking and rotting on the inside but nice and white on the outside. He even called them pits of snakes and vipers.

Those are words you can't Dodge.

He was downright cruel to only one group of people—the religious fools. So is it any wonder that these same fools drive you to drink?

Gandhi is famous for saying he'd be a Christian if it weren't for the Christians, and I felt the same way for a very long time. I finally had to take my eyes off of Jesus's so-called friends and put my eyes back on him to realize that the Christian brand we see today has almost nothing to do with the things Jesus had to say.

At all.

I could write an entire book on all the absurdities that make up Christianity today.

(Its title:) Who put the DUMB in Christendom?

Almost nothing in the mega-world of the infamous Christian pastor has anything at all to do with the heart of Jesus the Master. Instead those God-damned wealthy bastards put on a weekly show and bask in the glow of the worship of their mega-church fans as they sway to the music of their uber-hip bands. Then and only then, when the stupid sheep have been whipped into a worshipful squall, MegaMan gets up and pastorbates™ in front of us all.

And after his needs are completely met—when the checks are written and the tithes are paid—he's whisked off in his hundred-thousand dollar Mercedes to an elegant place where his lunch has been waiting, while the poor and destitute are ignored completely or told to wait . . . for the church sponsored Saturday soup kitchen . . . which is nearly a week away. And it's held off the premises to keep the undesirables at bay, far from our fancy centers of rich religion.

And absolutely none of this has anything to do with fishing . . .

for men.

Which is *all* that Jesus said we are to do. To go and love and give
and serve—to the last drop. Just like he did. For the *least* of these.
So very old school.

I understand his temple tantrum. I've had many of the same. And if
I hadn't learned a thing from Jesus—like forgiving idiots who
make your life a living hell—I would be serving life in prison,
playing hide the sausage with O.J. Simpson.

Turn the other cheek. Return good for evil.

I've got to keep reminding myself over and over of the things that
Jesus would teach . . . because prison would be cruel.

I've watched my share of Oz. And I'm no fool.

Dorothy was right. There is no place like home.

Forgive. It's not just a good idea. It's the law (of love).
And Jesus Christ . . . he wasn't kidding.

10.

The *Son of God*

and the **Son of a Bitch!**

Life's sweet ironies . . .

It's funny but sometimes no matter how clever you try to be, life often one-ups you.

Recently, my friend Tommy drove seven hours to help me move. And this move was one that I didn't wish on even my worst enemy as there were catwalks, open architectural stairwells and spiral staircases climbing three floors into the heavens. This was the sort of place you couldn't wait to move into and dreaded moving out of.

And on top of the cruel layout, we're also talking unwieldy and ridiculous items . . . like giant armoires, a 350-pound slushy machine (don't ask), the oddly shaped, extraordinarily top-heavy pinball machine . . . and a few other enormous and impractical items sure to break your back.

It's no wonder that none of my local friends offered to help. Only poor, unsuspecting Tommy who probably imagined a regular kind of move. You know, a few folding chairs, a card table and the obligatory ornamental lawn ball. What's that going to take, maybe about an hour?

I hated leaving the three-story glass loft in the arts district, but I was feeling it was time to put down some roots, invest in a home and finally be part of the lucrative world of real estate. Then all I'd need to do was make myself comfortable on the Adirondack furniture on the big old front porch, sit back with a perspiring mint julep, and watch the housing market disintegrate before my eyes. My timing is always impeccable.

After 17 hours of backbreaking labor in the God-awful humidity of the deep South, Tommy was ready for a little relaxation on my breezy and welcoming new front porch. This is the porch I'd always dreamed of. Spacious and inviting, begging for giant ferns to be hung from the beams, with gleaming hardwood floors . . . the perfect oasis on my little 75-year-old Craftsman bungalow.

So after the grueling move, my friend and I spent the rest of the weekend sitting on that porch talking for hours and hours about life, love and the contradictions and challenges associated with being human while attempting to embrace the divine. The ridiculous and the sublime—all wrapped up in this incredibly confusing, yet always invigorating journey of a lifetime.

The sad thing is, we rarely have any revolutionary epiphanies, only those thoughts that seem incredibly profound while smoking pot. You remember those conversations—where all of your stoner friends are in awe of your genius and divine inspiration and it's only because they're all higher than kites. Since we're God-fearing Christians living in the South, we don't "take pot" anymore and instead we settle for extended communion plowing through six or seven glasses of red wine—often bestowing upon us the same profound insights as those pot-smoking snowboarding heathens. No matter, really. Despite how clever we think we are—drunk, high or painfully sober—God always gets the last word and outdoes even our best arguments.

After the exhausting weekend, Tommy made the long drive back to his small town and returned to work on Monday morning only to be greeted by the obese and omni-sweating bald man who visits his office quarterly to check on the office equipment.

He usually greets Tommy with the suspect line, "Howdy, Tommy, I'm here to check out your equipment." Which ironically is then usually followed by some gay bashing religious rhetoric mined from years of being a faithful, though unfruitful Southern Baptist.

On this day the conversation was particularly offensive and office-equipment-guy began to pontificate on how terrible the church had become in recent years. Tommy, still riding high on the heady fumes of freedom that he finds in the company of faith-filled fags, was more than ready to take on any gay-bashing blows this large man would foolishly deliver.

"We're in a heap o' trouble young man. A heap o' trouble. The church is way too lenient these days—lettin' any and every form of sinner in through its doors. Why I recently heard of a church that openly accepts them Homosectials!"

"Really, what church is that? And when are services?" Tommy wanted to ask, but didn't.

"Yessiree! I tell you what, we can't be far from God's judgment and wrath when this sort of vermin is accepted in the holy church." No wonder we had 9-11 and the Katrina! Tommy was about to point out that if God was aiming to wipe out the sinners, he needed a lot more practice—one of the only places spared by Katrina was bawdy Bourbon Street and the French Quarter. But he thought his energy would be better spent elsewhere.

"It's strange that you should say that today," Tommy replied. "Because I just spent the entire weekend with a Christian friend who also happens to be gay. And the funny thing is, I never feel closer to God than when I spend time with him and his friends.

"Well son, that is impossible. *Impossible*." The fat man fumed. I think it may be fair to say he was sputtering.

"You can *not*, simply straight up can *not* be a Christian and a homosectial, young man. It doesn't work that way little missy!"

"Hmmm," Tommy pretended to be thinking aloud. "I've been around church-going people all my life, and yet I have never seen so much authentic love as I do from my gay Christian friend. And didn't Jesus say that his followers would be known by their love?"

"That is pure malarkey. You are twistin' the holy scriptures to make your point and the hell fires await those who mess with God's words. Don't you git it, young man . . . once you come into contact with the redeeming blood of Jesus you are no longer the same wretch-id person you was before you was saved. Sins you committed before you was saved are washed in the blood of Jesus and you can no longer participate in those things once you have become a blood-bought Son of God!"

"I see," Tommy began. His dangerous mind was now becoming fully engaged as he looked sideways at this large man. (Maybe because it was the only way to get all of him into his field of vision.)

"With all due respect, am I to understand that you no longer sin?" Tommy asked.

"Well, no I don't commit the same sins I used to commit fore I gave my life to Jesus. I been set free of my old sinful nature and I reckon I become a new cre-A-shun in Christ. Fer instance—I used to cuss like a sailor and Jesus done delivered me from that filthy habit and it's no longer a part of who I am. It's my old nature and it is washed in the blood—and I am truly free of that nasty old cussin'. Jesus has gone and washed out my mouth and I don't swear no more. In fact it would be impossible for me to live like I used to."

"Wow," Tommy feigned to be impressed. "Let me ask you this. Did you over-eat before you were saved?"

The man began to look a little uncomfortable in his sweating skin. "Well, yes, I did over-eat before I was saved. But what's that got to do with anything?"

"Do you over-eat now, maybe snack a little more than you should?"

"Well, yep, I guess I do." The man looked down at his morbid obesity, fidgeting as he adjusted his belt and hiked up his pants to cover a roll or two.

"Well, then you are living in sin. Everyone knows the Bible says that we are not to covet or be gluttonous. Gluttony is definitely a sin and you are clearly defiling your body which is the temple of the Holy Spirit, right?"

"Well, that is different!!" The man nearly shouted . . . then realized he was in the middle of a quiet office environment.

"It is different," Tommy replied. "Because it is *your* sin. So it's easy for you to find grace for yourself but not for the homosexual."

The man continued to sweat and squirm. Tommy didn't take a breath or let up, "How can you say that you no longer commit the same sins you used to before you were saved and yet you are fat?"

"You son of a *bitch!*" the fat man shouted at Tommy, his face all red and his eyes buggy and nervous. With that, the redeemed Son of God stormed off—leaving Tommy to wonder if maybe he had found the fat man's inner sailor.

And that can't be all bad . . . as it would explain the extra weight.

Making this poor, fat man less a sinner and more a saint.

Unless, of course that inner sailor happened to be gay.

That would be a different story.

11.

The
Peter Vision

This may scare the *sheet* out of you. I know it did me.

Leviticus 18:22 Thou shalt not lie with mankind, as with womankind: it is **abomination**. (KJV)

Abomination:

1. The feeling of extreme disgust and hatred; abhorrence; detestation; loathing; as, he holds tobacco in abomination.
2. That which is abominable; anything hateful, wicked, or shamefully vile; an object or state that excites disgust and hatred; a hateful or shameful vice; pollution.

(from www.wiktionary.org)

Well, it would seem that there isn't much more disgusting and abominable than those damn homosexuals—at least according to the fundies who like to paint obnoxious signs.

God
Hates Fags!

It has been made clear to me and most of my friends, through countless sermons that never seem to end, how offended God is at the heinous deeds of those filthy gays. Things they do in their bedrooms are things no one should ever say.

Much less do.

It's amazing how much attention the Christian right has given to this issue in light of the fact that it was a subject Jesus failed to mention. He was more concerned with love and a message of redemption.

But for some reason it's not uncommon to hear sermon after sermon of how much our loving God hates gays and how their expression of love for one another will be the one thing that brings our culture to its knees. Divorce—one of the things Jesus did point out was sin—is conveniently overlooked, but the trouble with preaching a sermon like that is that far fewer tithes would roll in. So we wink at the associate pastor and his lovely new wife. While we beat the homosexual within an inch of his wretched life.

Q: What gives?
A: (Divorced people.)

Despite all the hullabaloo surrounding the abominable homos and queers, there are only a handful of scriptures in the Bible that are responsible for creating all this fear.

And loathing.

I usually hate when authors use dictionary definitions to make their point, but in this case, I thought it important that we take this thing right down to the letter of the law, before injecting any sort of personal opinion on such a weighty matter. And it does matter. Untold thousands have lost their lives over laws and their misinterpretation or misapplication. And I'm talking universally here, not just the laws surrounding homosexuality.

If you're anything like me, you're not looking for someone to twist scripture and suggest alternate meanings to justify a behavior or a way of life. When I was younger, I always cringed when certain rainbow-waving theologians claimed that the verses found in Romans 1:26-27 were condemning the practice of having sex with male temple prostitutes, not denouncing a committed, monogamous same sex relationship. That may be true, but I'm not convinced.

Leviticus 18:22 made it pretty clear that it was impossible to be queer and please God. ("Do not have sexual relations with a man as one does with a woman; that is detestable.") And that was enough to ensure me a lifetime of guilt and shame. Every time I found myself wanting to enter the gay relationship game, these words would echo in the hollow halls of my fractured mind. What's a boy to do when he wants to do—boys?

But in reality, there are a huge number of other laws that are ignored wholesale by Christians and the church at large, while all the fire and brimstone preaching and gnashing is reserved almost exclusively for gay-bashing.

An A.D.D. Insert.

This morning I received an email from Jeremy
in L.A., and he was screaming how much
West Hollywood needs Gay Conversations
With God. Suddenly the urgency hit me.
There are people dying by the roadside. Gays
everywhere are like partial birth abortions . . .
boys and girls who made it out of the womb,
only to be mutilated and partially
slaughtered by churches and pastors who
have left them hanging on by a thread . . .
not really living, bleeding all over the place.

Then those pastors and leaders and holier-
than-thou types are screaming. (*"Get out of*

my church you filthy swine—you are getting
blood all over my shrine.")

Did you get that? *"My shrine."*
Not God's.

And these poor bleeding, brutalized sons and
daughters of the Most High God are living
out their desolate heritages—because no one
told them that they are, in fact, heirs.

Heirs—sons and daughters of the most high
who now are living like swine.

And then judged and punished for doing so.

Since so many tears have been shed over the tragedies that have
unfolded over the interpretations of biblical laws, I thought maybe
a little humor could put us in better spirits as we ready ourselves
for a little Peter Vision:

A few years ago Dr. Laura was doing some horrific gay bashing on
her popular syndicated radio advice show. She made it clear where
these despicable homos were going to go after they died.

Someone with a brilliant mind and a little time wrote the following
open letter to Dr. Laura, which appears in numerous places on the
Internet (and is immortalized on Snopes.com). Really, I can't thank
them enough for this simple missive that helps me be more dismis-
sive of all those who love to build a doctrine or denomination on a
single scripture from their own interpretation.

Here is that letter of the law:

Dear Dr. Laura,

Thank you for doing so much to educate people regarding God's law. I have learned a great deal from you, and I try to share that knowledge with as many people as I can. When someone tries to defend the homosexual lifestyle, for example, I simply remind him that Leviticus 18:22 clearly states it to be an abomination. End of debate.

I do need some advice from you, however, regarding some of the specific laws and how to best follow them.

When I burn a bull on the altar as a sacrifice, I know it creates a pleasing odor for the Lord (Lev. 1:9). The problem is my neighbors. They claim the odor is not pleasing to them. How should I deal with this?

I would like to sell my daughter into slavery, as it suggests in Exodus 21:7. In this day and age, what do you think would be a fair price for her?

Lev. 25:44 states that I may buy slaves from the nations that are around us. A friend of mine claims that this applies to Mexicans but not Canadians. Can you clarify. Why can't I own Canadians?

I have a neighbor who insists on working on the Sabbath. Exodus 35:2 clearly states he should be put to death. Am I morally obligated to kill him myself?

A friend of mine feels that even though eating shellfish is an abomination (Lev. 20:25), it is a lesser abomination than homosexuality. I don't agree. Can you settle this?

Lev. 21:20 states that I may not approach the altar of God if I have a defect in my sight. I have to admit that I wear reading glasses. Does my vision have to be 20/20, or is there some wiggle room here?

Most of my male friends get their hair trimmed, including the hair around their temples, even though this is expressly forbidden by Leviticus 19:27. How should they die?

My uncle has a farm. He violates Leviticus 19:19 by planting two different crops in the same field—as does his wife by wearing garments made of two different kinds of thread (a cotton/poly blend). He also tends to curse and blaspheme a lot. Is it really necessary that we go to all the trouble of getting the whole town together to stone them (Leviticus 24:10-16)? Couldn't we just burn them to death at a private family affair like we do with people who sleep with their in-laws? (Leviticus 20:14)

I know you have studied these things extensively, so I am confident you can help. Thank you again for reminding us that God's word is eternal and unchanging.

I don't think any additional commentary is needed. This incredible letter does with simple humor what would take pages and pages of discourse to make the same sort of point.

But the problem still remains. What do we do with the handful of verses that prescribe heinous curses on my brothers and sisters who can't even think straight? I, for one, became exhausted by the question posed by the thousands who wrote me emails after my first books hit the shelves. These were God's precious kids who were hating themselves—because of the things they'd been told by pastors and bastards and catholic headmasters, not to mention the evangelists and the lay people, who have no trouble laying people as long as they are of the opposite sex.

I was vexed.

I finally came to a point in my life where I'd had enough and I pretty much had it out with God. I looked to the heavens from my little beach bungalow in Laguna—and I demanded that God tell me the truth. Is it a sin to be gay? What do I do with these scriptures? I'm tired of not knowing what to say . . . when your children come to me on the verge of tears or even suicide. I am sick and tired of being denied a straight answer to this gay question. I am not moving until you tell me what I need to know.

An A.D.D. Moment.

Moses was the first person to coin the term "Over my dead body." He used it on God to overrule something heinous he planned to do to the Children of Israel and most of the adults. I personally don't think that would be a phrase I'd use when dealing with the one who could easily take you up on your offer. But one of the cool things about God is—he admires people with balls. Even when those people are acting a little off the wall. So he changed his plans and spared Moses's life. How nice. (See Exodus 32.)

For a while nothing seemed to be happening. There was only silence after my little tantrum, so I sat back in the couch and looked longingly out at the vastness of the sea. The great space that exists between who we are and who we want to be. Despite my angry outburst I was in that soft, liminal sand—ready to be shaped by God's loving hands.

The sun was beginning to set, and the palms made for a gorgeous silhouette. In the silence I reached for my New Testament and flipped the pages open to wherever they happened to land. And I began to read—

A little Acts to grind . . .

Acts 10:9—

Peter went up on the roof to pray. He became hungry and wanted something to eat, and while the meal was being prepared, he fell into a trance.

He saw heaven opened and something like a large sheet being let down to earth by its four corners. It contained all kinds of four-footed animals, as well as reptiles of the earth and birds of the air.

Then a voice told him, "Get up, Peter. Kill and eat."

"Surely not, Lord!" Peter replied. "I have never eaten anything impure or unclean. "The voice spoke to him a second time, "Do not call anything impure that God has made clean." This happened three times, and immediately the sheet was taken back to heaven.

I had read this verse a thousand times before. And I had also sat in church services where this passage had been read to begin a celebration of how this incredible vision was the invitation to the outsiders—the abominable Gentiles who had been despised by the Jews. This was the welcome mat that God himself had used to welcome the hated into his fold.

(And these God-damned Gentiles were not in the habit of abiding by the laws of the Jewish land. Yet God was reaching out his hand—to welcome them in—in spite of their despicable foreskin and ongoing "sin".)

Undoubtedly some of you haven't heard these tired verses before. So let me put them into context. Back in the day the kosher Jews would not eat anything that was considered to be an abomination or unclean. That meant pork, shellfish and venison were completely off limits. If you were to witness another Jew order a delightful shrimp cocktail, say, at happy hour or a bar-mitzvah—you would know exactly what to do! You would throw his ass out and he would be an abomination, unholy, unclean and worthy of death. At the very least, he would be dead to his fellow Jews.

The kosher dietary laws were the most important laws of their day, and since there was no such thing as refrigeration or the FDA, it was crucial for the Israeli population to follow these laws to stay healthy and free of unnecessary disease. It seems these would be good guidelines to have in place as a survival mechanism for a small group of people with global aspirations. A group that seemed to anger every other nation and cause God himself no end of consternation . . . but, strangely, they were, in fact, God's chosen nation.

But as I was reading about the Peter vision—the event that took place while Peter was praying on the roof, it dawned on me. God changed the rules in the middle of the game and this was a game where nothing else had changed. Sub-Zeros didn't suddenly appear on the scene, and devices that could eradicate trichinosis in those filthy swine would not be around for a long, long time.

I asked God what in the world he could be thinking. Had he started drinking? Here was a law that God himself had put in place and it had long been the centerpiece for his kosher chosen race. Men and women had been defined by what they put in their mouths for a long time and suddenly God decides to cook up a little schnitzel, then tell Peter, "It's dinner time."

This vision Peter had while praying on the roof was revolutionary in that particular place at that particular time, and it didn't make any sense to the Jews who didn't happen to be on that roof when Peter heard God say "Do not call anything impure that God has made clean."

Bam. Then it hit me.

God wanted a relationship with the millions upon millions who would never be able to abide by that rigid Jewish law. So he changed the rules in the middle of the game in order to embrace all those who were unwilling to be tamed.

God broke the rule to welcome outsiders in. Even though the outsiders were known for their blatant sin.

I asked God if my assessment of this situation was in fact true?

And without further ado . . .

I felt a wave of God's undeniable love and the assurance that this was the reason for this unexpected change of plans. He was more concerned with being in a relationship with his sons and daughters than he was about the law. So he got rid of the law to open up the door for a relationship with millions and millions more.

Then I pressed him further. "Is this what you're doing now with your kids who happen to be gay?" And these are the words I clearly heard God say: "I am more concerned with where my children will spend eternity and less with where they spend the night. Let no man call unclean what I call clean today."

This was completely unexpected. It took me a moment to realize that I had not been neglected. God finally—and clearly—answered my question about this gay thing after all.

I know for a fact that there must have been a hell storm when Peter announced his new information to the uptight leaders of God's chosen nation.

Guess what, you silly Sadducee—shrimp scampi
is now abomination free!
(Still pretty high in cholesterol though.
Moderation is the key!)

And the reaction today would be the same. Men and women insist that God will never change. And more importantly, he will never change his mind. In fact scripture shows over and over how his prophets and his priests often helped him change his mind—and he chooses mercy over judgment almost every single time.

I will never understand the difference between the God of the Old Testament who seems to be full of piss and vinegar and fire-and-brimstone wrath; and the God of the New Testament who no longer seems to suggest those horrifying blood baths.

The New Testament God suggests turning the other cheek and he makes it perfectly clear that if you wish to inherit the earth you must first become meek. No longer is it an eye for an eye and a tooth for a tooth. And gone are the days when you bash in the heads of the Babylonian youth.

This is a new age.

And today is a brand new day. No matter what anyone has to say, I clearly understood what God was communicating to me—in his inimitable way—in Laguna Beach. There is a whole giant tribe of his children that he is dying to reach. And he died—to reach.

This is a God whose mercies are new every morning. This is a God of compassion and love who is not eager to throw his misguided into the lakes of fire just because you invoked his ire. Those are the sentiments of angry old men who can't get control of the situation they are in . . .

. . . so they condemn innocent men.
This, however is a God of love. He always was.

A God who lives, loves, serves and gives.

To the last drop.

This is a God who is in fact holy—and it is *his* holiness that saves us, not ours.

And for those who will fight this with all their hearts—those who will cringe at the possibility that God may not in fact hate fags—I think it may be time that you go and pack your bags. Because God isn't needing your services any longer. Do I need to say this any stronger?

Drop your weapons, your venom and your sermons of hate . . .

If I were you, I wouldn't stand in God's way.

He is rolling out a red carpet (a carpet he paid for with his life) to welcome all of his children in— to enjoy the rich inheritance that has been reserved for all of them—all who are willing to believe.

For those with open hands willing to receive.

God's free gift.

Allow the great God of the Universe to replace your hearts of stone—with tender hearts of flesh.

For this is an awesome God of love—and you ain't seen nothing yet. (Sorry, a Palin moment.)

I'm not suggesting that you sin with reckless abandon—or even that homosexuality is no longer a sin. That isn't my place—in fact it's way above my pay grade.

I'm just telling you what I heard when I asked God to fill me in.

Do what you will with what I've shared. But one thing is for certain. Lives will be spared.

And love will be shared.
Bigotry, prejudice and hatred will cease.

And millions of those who were once denied, once despised, beaten to death or within an inch of their lives . . . will now be sitting at Jesus's feet.

And not a single word will be spoken. There will be no need. He will pull his beloved child close. He will pull you close.

And weep.

And weep.

And weep.

12.

imMobile
in Mobile.

(Alabama that is.)

Engaging God's special forces who have been disqualified,
by believing the lie.

I think it would take the dead coming back to life to lure me to
spend any time at all in Alabama. And come to think of it, that is
exactly what happened. While working in television, I was covering the incredible story of a two-year-old boy who had inadver-
tently fallen into the swimming pool at a day care. WTF?? A swimming pool at a day care? It was Alabama—no further questions. It
so happened that this little boy was the *second* to fall in the pool
that very day. The first was saved. Nobody noticed the second until
it was too late.

This incredible little boy was declared dead more than once. The
third time, the death certificate was signed and he had been packed
on ice for more than five hours while they prepared to harvest his
organs to parcel them out to other little children in grave need. The
parents, unbelievably faith-filled, loving human beings stood at
their lifeless little boy's side, praying in the face of death—that
God would change his mind.

And he did. He sometimes does, you know.

Five hours after this little boy had been declared dead by the powers that be, a greater power that none of us can see—unless you are willing to believe—kicked into overdrive in that E.R. and this little dead boy wiggled his nose and opened his eyes. His purple and black complexion turned instantly to lily white. The mother ran screaming from the hospital room, shouting, "My boy is alive, my boy is alive." Hospital personnel tried to quiet this hysterical woman, assuring her that this was impossible but a normal mistake for a grieving and distraught mother to make.

Then a nurse witnessed the movement and saw the open eyes and she joined this jubilant mother making loud exuberant cries. The two of them ran down the hall summoning everyone who would come to witness this miracle. A lifeless boy—was now alive. And tears of joy filled his parents eyes.

Even God cries. He really does, you know.

(And strangely enough he, too, had a son who defeated death and returned to life.)

All of this took place while this little boy's brother had been in the hospital's chapel praying that God would give him a chance to say goodbye. But God did one even better. He allowed this faith-filled 11-year-old to look his brother in the eye and welcome him back home. After hearing this incredible story first-hand, I would have to say that my faith has grown.

So it was a resurrection that took me to Alabama. And after checking into the beautiful Victorian B&B in the long row of Mobile's famous homes, I learned that these old painted beauties had a resurrection story of their own. Back when Martin Luther King Jr. was assassinated at the Lorraine Motel in Memphis Tennessee, the South went up in flames. Rioting, looting and mayhem ensued. The southern whites knew exactly what they needed to do. They left . . . in order to survive.

And they left their glorious mansions behind—in order to save their lives. These big old beauties went from being opulent homes filled with warmth of flickering fires, ample love and stories of their own—to being vacuous, lifeless old eyesores that were falling into disrepair.

And no one even cared.

Finally some people with vision, passion and courage decided to push past their fear and breathe life back into this boulevard of broken dreams—where all these behemoths were rotting and dying alongside of the road. One by one, new life has come and Government Street is now even further proof that the dead can come back to life with a little faith and a putty knife.

(And a million hours of grueling labor and a hundred cans of paint.)

I learned all of this from the innkeeper at one of these resurrected Victorian gems, and I must say that although this man was friendly enough—he answered all of my questions and gave me directions to the little bistros and the hot spots for Mobile's vibrant gay life—something didn't seem quite right. I generally throw out some spiritual conversation starters to determine if someone is open to those things. This guy ignored all of them flatly and when I looked him in the eyes there was an intangible lifelessness—a hollowness where I expected to find a soul. Something was missing, but I couldn't quite place it—maybe it was just me that he didn't like. So I let it go.

The next morning while at breakfast I felt that God wanted me to engage him, even though I was exhausted from a grueling day of shooting and a tumultuous sleepless night. Come on God, give me a break, I would love to just sit quietly and eat in peace. And this guy clearly doesn't like me so pass the bacon grease.

(And trust me, there was a lot of that in every dish except the fruit.)

So I looked up at our host and told him I wanted to know everything there was to know about his background, about his story . . . about his life. And for fun, I said:

"And be graphic!"

And then it happened. I don't know what it was—maybe it was the fact that someone was showing genuine interest in him, in his heart. Perhaps he hadn't been engaged like that in years. Whatever the case, his eyes lit up and suddenly he came alive. "Oh my God, now I know where I recognize you from! Of course," he said with genuine excitement and surprise. "Didn't you host the *700 Club* years ago from time to time?"

Now I was shocked. "Yes . . . but . . . ?" I stopped myself short while my mind raced. He'd been so difficult to engage in topics of spirituality—how on earth would he have ever seen . . . " Before I could finish the thought, he interrupted. "Oh my God, I used to watch that show religiously! And you would be on every once in a while giving reports from around the world. Am I right?"

This dead man walking had suddenly come back to life—his face had a brand new light and real joy registered in his eyes. I almost didn't recognize him. But his resurrection recharged me and my interest in him was now completely authentic. I wanted to know everything.

For the next two hours Derek began to recount a most unexpected tale of his former life. He walked me through his powerful salvation story—how he came to know Christ and how that dramatically changed his life. He even told me how he had been filled by the Holy Spirit while "taking a dump" in the second floor bathroom of his college campus (that definitely was T.M.I.).

I guess I did say, "Be graphic." This certainly wasn't what I had in mind.

But he was energized and although I didn't want to picture that Holy Spirit encounter in a public bathroom, I knew that the telling of this story was actually building his faith and bringing him back to life. And what's more, he was opening up my eyes.

Derek continued to surprise me when he told how he had been given many powerful gifts from God himself. There were occasions where he prayed for the sick and they were healed and a blind girl was given back her sight. He was being used powerfully—and I pictured this big bearish guy as one of God's very special forces—like a Navy SEAL (complete with whiskers and lots of fur). When he finished telling me all the miracles he'd witnessed and how he'd been enlisted in God's service for so many years, I couldn't help but notice his eyes had filled with tears.

Though he had almost forgotten—God hadn't.

And this was a special son.

I looked up at Derek's big old teary eyes and I couldn't help but ask him what happened. What was he doing in Mobile, Alabama, working in this bed and breakfast making bacon and fresh Southern egg pies?

His face darkened as a cloud threatened to extinguish some of his newly found light. "I'm hiding from God." He looked up sheepishly from the maple syrup tureen. The sweet sticky liquid was dripping down the side and pooling on the glistening table—that Derek had meticulously polished and kept eternally pristine.

"Well, I think he's found you, my friend." I could feel God's love pooling in my eyes—filling my heart with warmth that I hadn't felt for this man before.

I then asked Derek if it would be okay for me to pray for him—it says that we are to stir up the gift in one another by the laying on of hands. That we are to call the forth the gifts in each other that have gone dormant, those things that have died. And I knew in this moment—this sacred moment—that this son had been disqualified.

And he had done that to himself.

He had been told by so many for so many years that he was a sinner . . .

. . . and God couldn't possibly use queers.

I asked Derek if he was gay when all of these miracles were happening in his life? He smiled uncomfortably and said "Of course," but no one knew it back in the day. I reminded him that God did—and he still chose to use him—even though he was fully aware of everything that he did, with other men or in the darkened corners of his mind.

I told him, "The closet isn't dark enough to keep God from knowing your secrets, and yet, the miracles flourished. They only stopped because you *thought* you were disqualified."

So this sidelined son, one of God's special forces, abandoned his powerful guns and decided to hide out in Mobile Alabama in shame.

This once vibrant man was plodding joylessly to his grave.

And lives that he was called to reach—those he was called to touch—those that he should heal—were also bleeding and dying by the side of the road. There could be no greater waste, no greater shame. A spiritual Katrina has devastated much of our world and there is no more time to waste. I stopped my prayer and looked Derek squarely in the eye.

"You know, it's time. Time that you pick up where you left off—and bring life and healing to those who are bleeding and burdened and dying inside. You hold the keys to freedom, to joy to health and spiritual wealth. Yet you are sharing them with no one—and in the process you are killing yourself."

And right there in Mobile, Alabama, on the very street where the giant Victorians had come back to life, I believe I was witnessing another resurrection right before my eyes. This disqualified son who had become dead to his faith was now filling back up with joy and light. And maybe even the realization that he was more than qualified.

He was a treasured son of the Most High.

On my flight home I began to think about the tragedy that this self-disqualification has brought upon this earth. Much of it comes from those God-damned signs that tell wicked lies that God hates his kids who are not quite right.

But that is why the first resurrection took place. God's own son took our own place—so that death would be defeated once and for all—and God's broken, wounded children would be able to live rich lives shameless, healed, and standing tall.

Not penance, church attendance or even obeying every letter of the law. Nothing we do, nothing we say and no matter how spit polished and pressed we appear to be—would make any difference at all.

That would make his free gift of no effect—and that sublime gift is what saves those foolish enough to believe. If you can believe this—then you ain't seen *nothing* yet. (As they say in the South—and Southern Alaska.)

I want to be foolish enough to be used in any way that God sees fit. If it is simply calling out the troops that have fallen in the ditch . . .

. . . but even better if he wants to use me to raise the dead.

I know an army exists and could be Mobilized in Alabama and beyond—all in the twinkling of an eye—and all it will take is a seed of faith and the willingness to believe that you are not disqualified.

Let the revolution begin.

There's a world of hurt and we are running out of time.

13.

The Naked Truth.

Prophet, Priest or Whore

As I begin to write this chapter my heart is aching as I think about the grave injustices that have been done to some of God's most beautiful children. I used to think that the inquisition was a dark time until I started to rehearse some of the horrific travesties that are being done right now in an enlightened world by enlightened peoples who claim to carry the light of God's love.

Legend of a fall . . .

From time to time I book massages to take care of some lower back issues from a terrible horseback riding accident I suffered several years ago while trying to impress a date. Somewhere in the middle of this equestrian fantasy where I thought I must be looking a lot like Brad Pitt in *Legends of the Fall*, the horse lost its mind I lost my balance and was dragged for a hundred yards, only to fall out of my stirrup and have the horse double back and stomp my spine. It was a legendary fall . . . and the pain was excruciating.

Speaking of stallions, when I was about to get on the massage table I noticed that the young male therapist I booked (did I mention he was Italian?) was removing his clothes as well. I figure if I'm going to spend the money on a massage I may as well have someone beautiful do the work. It's a weakness—one I may have to address. But when I saw Jordan's body, I didn't protest the fact that he'd gotten rid of all his clothes. I think it was because I was so intrigued by what was unfolding before me, and although it was not my intent to have a sexual encounter, there was something exciting about the fact that I didn't know what was about to happen. I tried to justify it, thinking it may be this young man's technique. And somehow, in a twisted fashion I could claim innocence in it all.

(And we could both turn the other cheeks.)

My heart began to race as he started working on my feet. I realized that all I'd have to do is lift my head, turn around, and I'd see one of the most beautiful beings on the planet in all his glory. But then something happened. Something bigger and more beautiful than Jordan. In the middle of our conversation, the subject of God came up and instead of this being a therapeutic session for my body, I realized that I was in the middle of a therapeutic session for this man's soul. (And, perhaps mine.)

As soon as Jordan realized that although I was gay, I had come to a place where I understood God to be my Father and friend, he began to pour out the rest of his story. In a few minutes I realized that as stunning as Jordan was on the outside, he had a heart that eclipsed even his physical beauty

"You know, I was a Christian for a big part of my life," Jordan admitted as he worked on my calf muscles. "I was in love with Jesus and was a member of a Pentecostal church in Florida on track to become a minister of music. That was until some married dude in the church told me he could help me with my music career and he ended up fucking me instead."

"You mean, he fucked you over?" I asked.

"No, I wish that were the case. He literally fucked me. I was only

17 and still believed he would do something to help my career so I went along with it for a while, but then I realized I was being used. So I reported the whole thing to the church leadership and you know what happened? I was kicked out of the choir and kicked out of the church. He fucked an underage boy and should have gone to prison and I was the one who was punished. What sense does that make? God-damned religion."

As Jordan relayed the story I could see a glimpse of that tender heart that had so desperately wanted to be healed and helped. The broken boy who wanted more than anything to please his God and find peace with this turmoil that was raging inside of him. He explained that although he was forced to leave his church family and friends, he was referred to another church where he could get some help and maybe even deliverance for this horrific disease or demonic infestation of his.

Unfortunately Jordan was violated yet again. The new pastor built a level of trust and a sense of safety for Jordan, but failed to mention his own struggle with same sex attraction and he ended up using Jordan for his own prurient purposes. This young man who loved Jesus and wanted only to please him by being a music minister and using his gifts to affect others was so disillusioned, so devastated that he ended up leaving home at a young age only to create his own happy ending. So to speak.

Jordan is a survivor. He learned the art of massage and then realized that there was more money in the art of sensual and erotic massage. And although some would call him a prostitute for using his body for monetary gain, you didn't have to look very hard to see that this man's heart remained soft, broken and malleable despite the painful journey he'd been on.

The conversation became heated and electric and because we were both naked it was surreal. I found myself speaking with the same passion I speak with on my tours for previous books—and almost forgot the insanity of the situation. Jordan asked a million questions about my understanding of God and how to deal with the whole gay thing. He asked whether it was bad that he was a go-go dancer for a fetish show.

I told him God only knows.

Some of the questions were not easy to answer. But one thing was clear to me. This was a beloved son. A son who had been abused by self-proclaimed Godly men—men who should have been more interested in holding Jordan's heart than his cock.

These were men who were living in such denial over their own struggle with their sexuality that they abused the innocence of a beautiful young man on a spiritual journey only to leave him bleeding and dying by the road. A road that would ultimately lead him away from a real relationship with the Man who couldn't love him more—into hundreds of broken relationships with other broken men where he would have to sell his body in order to save his soul.

My anger toward Christians and the way they have handled the whole homosexuality thing nearly reached the boiling point all over again as Jordan continued his heart-breaking story. Thoughts of revenge rolled around in my head and I was reminded of why so many warm, spiritual, loving gay people suddenly become venomous at the mere mention of God.

Then, thankfully, another voice, a voice that was not my own, pushed its way to the front of my thoughts. "You are not unlike the pastors that you are condemning. You were distracted by Jordan's physical beauty and you were willing to selfishly let things take their course when you could have honored him as my son—and seen past his sensuality into his sensitive warm heart. Jordan longs for intimacy and it has been sexualized on his broken path and that is why he dropped his clothes when he felt the warmth coming from your heart. You could have been a bigger man by not allowing him to be exposed. You could have invited warmth and intimacy and shown him it was possible while wearing clothes."

It was then that I realized that my harsh judgment on those pastors was now the standard by which I was judged. Suddenly Jesus's words, "Judge not, lest you be judged" had a whole new meaning for me. Thankfully for us, however, ours is not a God who thrives on judgment, he is a God who breathes both grace and love. Even though I felt some well-earned shame, God didn't need or want to rub my nose in my mistake. But he did need to show me that I didn't have the right to judge the misdeeds of those men before—I, too, am capable of being a pious judgmental pastor and I'm also capable of being a whore.

God's message was clear as the massage was coming to an end. Despite the way things had begun, I was able to honor Jordan as one of God's sons and instead of using him for pleasure I could now celebrate him as my brother and my friend.

And there was a happy ending to our time together, although not the kind you might have imagined.

An authentic Happy Ending

Jordan and I talked for another two hours after our session. He played me his inspired music—the stuff he had created after leaving the church. He wrote, produced and played all the instruments as well as doing all the vocal work himself. His talent was outstanding and it was clear that God's promise that the gifts he gives to us are not taken away—no matter what we do with them or how we choose to live our lives. He is a good father and he isn't petty or precious with his gifts. They are freely given and no matter what others may do or others may say—this is a God who is good for his word no matter how we choose to play the game.

Jordan explained the divine timing in our meeting as he had come to a place in the last few days where he'd decided it may be time to give up on God altogether. He had been studying Scientology and although he didn't see it as a religion he was coming to understand that he could be his own power and source and would not need to lean on anyone else. Including God.

"I can't thank you enough for everything you have given me today. Everything you said made complete sense and I realize that I don't have to give up on God—and I don't want to. Because he hasn't given up on me."

And despite the fact that I knew better and didn't intervene when the massage was headed east—like Jordan I realized that God wasn't going to give up on me and he never, ever will as long as we ask him for forgiveness and continue to believe.

We are going to make mistakes a million times along the way—and as much as I would love to be above the fascination of illicit sex and sensual connections, I now know that God will offer his protection—if we remain in a place of openness and trust.

Final Judgment

Despite all the signs and sermons, both live and via satellite, that claim that the hottest fires in hell are reserved for godless sodomites, I think we may all end up a little bit surprised when we stand before our God naked on that final day. Although some claim it will be the prostitutes or perverts who receive God's harshest wrath—and others like myself believe cruel and pious pastors will be tormented in an eternal fiery bath—I now realize the greatest peril awaits the most horrific criminal of all—and that criminal could be me when I choose to judge anyone at all.

After my very real run-in with my own frailty and weakness, I cannot remain in a place of being judge and jury—as I myself will encounter hell's own fury. The thing I can do is choose to forgive the pastors, priests and prophets who have broken their sacred trust and have perverted what once was holy and exchanged real love for lust.

I remain amazed at how many Jordans there are in this world. I am sickened when I think about how many beautiful sons and daughters have been discarded, damaged and destroyed by the scriptures that are misinterpreted and fired as deadly missiles at God's sons and daughters—those that were already bleeding and in pain and left for dead along the way.

There are painful consequences for these actions and many young lives will never be the same. Those who once held so much promise now live lives steeped in quiet shame.

There is nothing we can do about those things that have been done. But together we can choose to forgive all those who may have personally brought us pain. And realize that no matter if those crimes were committed under the banner of God's name—his heart is broken by injustice and he offers us real healing in his warm embrace. And God-sized tears are streaming down this Father's face.

For us to authentically move forward in our journey we will have to rise to a new place—we will have to become bigger than those who hurt us, bigger than those who judged us, bigger than the pain.

And by choosing to inhabit this large land of true forgiveness, we'll be ambassadors of grace.

As we go forward in our journey encountering injustice of all kinds, I wonder if it is possible to choose love, grace and forgiveness over judgment every time.

Another A.D.D. Moment

A friend recently read this chapter and was confused by how I had gotten into this situation in the first place. None of it made any sense to him. As we talked through his questions, I realized that at the time of this massage I was trying to sublimate my sexuality—by living in a way that would keep me from having an authentic relationship with another man. So to meet my need for touch I would consciously or subconsciously book massages that could turn into more. So in my attempt to please God by being celibate, I made myself an "acceptable" whore. Even in writing this chapter, I wasn't able to admit to you that this sort of massage wasn't out of the norm. I had learned how to read between the lines and book therapists who may just cross the line. This kind of helps bring more understanding for the Swaggarts and Haggards of our time, even pedophiliac priests. Our sexuality has to go somewhere. Why not live and love authentically, instead of settling for what seems to be acceptable—though twisted, fleeting and cheap?

14.
Corpus Christi.

Change *please*!

Holy Shit!

That pretty much sums up Terrence McNally's outrageously moving play, *Corpus Christi*. It's an unusual mix of hedonism, biblical passages, absurdity and profound truths. But the most amazing thing about this crazy presentation of the Gospel message where Jesus is a gay boy growing up in Corpus Christi, Texas, in the '50s is the fact that during the performance, God just happens to show up. I mean, he really shows up. It's a cameo of sorts—but lucky for the actors he doesn't upstage anyone. Instead he uplifts them and I honestly believe he breathes through them allowing us—the audience—to feel his tangible presence in the theater. This is yet another instance where God chooses to show up in the least likely of places and speak through the least likely to reach those he loves with all his heart.

This is the same play that met with death threats, bomb threats and protestors from churches all over New York. These warriors of God forgot to allow the play to open before they came to a decision—and they moved *in faith* believing that any piece of art depicting Jesus in any form or fashion other than the way they were convinced he had appeared would have to be a perversion of the Gospel and was worth fighting for. Maybe even worth killing for.

Funny. It's pretty much the same group of protestors Jesus encountered a few thousand years ago when his passion play opened off, off, off Broadway in the backside of bumfuck Egypt on a small stage in a barn under one stellar spotlight that happened to be run by God himself. This little light not only illuminated the actor as he made his way onto the earth's stage—but it also served as one of those fancy sweeping gala lights that criss-cross the heavens to alert everyone that there is a major event happening and it would be important to drop whatever it is you're doing and make your way to the opening.

A few wise men took note of the light show and made their way to the rude carpet of sand and dust, soiled by the animals that shared the little theater in Bethlehem. Humble, for sure, but in essence, this was quite the production. It had been years in the making and the script and pre-production had been worked over and over by prophets and seers who would pen how this humble savior would make his grand entrance in the least likely of stages, to the least likely audience. And like Terrence McNally's play—this opening was met with death threats as well.

It turns out that in Jesus's time, those who were in the seats of power were threatened by what may possibly happen in that little theater of the absurd—even before the performance began. Herod was hell-bent on stopping this production and he instructed his men to find out where this little play was going to take place and kill the star before he could make curtain call.

It was the same for Moses—yet another powerful force who was sent to help set God's people free. Those in power got wind of the coming revolution and the death threats turned into death squads and all male infants were mercilessly drowned in the Nile, to put a stop to the madness that Moses would bring to this earth. Madness that took the shape of freedom for countless thousands of God's chosen people. And once again—death threats were no match for God's plan. Thankfully, in the case of Jesus and in the case of Moses—the show did go on.

And the performances were spectacular. Sure, they had their share of bad reviews but for the most part these two powerful actors overcame all odds and were able to show the world the power that happens when you are willing to step into the role that God has cast you in and play the part with conviction and courage—no matter what the right and the religious have to say. Bombs or no bombs—the play must go on.

And that was exactly the case for Terrence McNally when *Corpus Christi* was about to open at the prestigious Manhattan Theatre Club. A band of mercenaries who took it upon themselves to hold a little inquisition of their own to defend the faith put out such a frightening array of threats that the theater ultimately pulled the performance and decided it would be safer for everyone if Mr. McNally kept his little message to himself.

But God has a way of working around death threats when he has something to say with life and death urgency. So when prolific, Pulitzer Prize-winning playwright Tony Kushner learned that *Corpus Christi* was going to be pulled from the theater before it ever opened, he made a death threat of his own. He told the theater that if they pulled *Corpus Christi*, he would be forced to pull all of his plays from their stage, and they could never again feature any of his work. This got the attention of the board—who suddenly realized that the show must go on.

Thank God for the Angels in America.

And it is a crazy show. A show that could send a right wing Christian into cardiac arrest. Even the most liberal of believers will find him or herself wondering at points if it is okay to laugh—when the baby Jesus is being thrown around the stage like a football—or when Jesus and Judas are making out at the high school prom.

I like to think that I'm not religious anymore, but I found myself uncomfortable at so many points in this show. I had pretty much hit the full range of emotions within the first 15 minutes—the opening baptism scene brought tears to my eyes and a joy I hadn't felt in a long, long time. Then in the bawdy scenes where Jesus was being molested by a football coach and priest I found myself appalled—thinking that there is no way that Jesus could have been molested and why would the playwright even suggest it.

Then my ignorance became painfully obvious to me . . . and I noticed that my old-time religion was still eclipsing my vision, no matter how many times I tried to exorcise myself from the hideousness of it all.

Then, like a single star in the night sky—I discovered a brilliant Truth.

Jesus had been beaten up. He had his head shoved in a toilet and flushed repeatedly for being gay. Just like in McNally's play. He was mocked by his peers at homecoming and instead of being voted most likely to succeed he was voted "most likely to take it up the Hershey highway." He was assaulted by older boys at the urinal for staring—and he was treated like shit by the PE teachers and coaches who loved to taunt the weaker boys who didn't seem to have the natural gift for the sports they preferred.

Jesus had experienced all of these things—portrayed upon on this stage. His abusive father abandoned him, his boozy old flirt of a mother fondled his privates and stole from him the right to have his own thoughts or harbor his own dreams. He had even been called "faggy Langteaux" in the halls of Liberty High School by farm boys who hated that he was different.

Yes—all of this and so much more had been done to Jesus and continues to be done to him. He said that whatever you do for the least of these—you do for me. And I always read and heard that in a positive light. That when I gave the homeless guy on the curb the

85 cents he asked for I was giving Jesus some cash for a malt liquor or pack of smokes.

But as I sat in the tiny theater on Melrose watching the incredible West Hollywood cast tell the Jesus story in a whole new light, all over again, I had a massive revelation.

Whatever you do for the least of these . . . whatever you do to the least of these you do to me. When a priest rapes a nine-year-old innocent boy, he rapes Jesus. When I look at a website where a young man is being humiliated in exchange for a few hundred dollars—I'm humiliating Jesus. When I give the homeless guy 85 cents, I have not given Jesus the money he needed to buy a decent meal, maybe a warmer jacket or perhaps a place to sleep that night.

And I, in my holy self-piousness have decided—by withholding my generosity—to keep him locked in a place of addiction where, in an attempt to stave off the cold for lack of proper clothing or the lack of proper shelter, he must settle instead for a cheap high that comes in a large bottle—a high that will take the edge off—a high that will dull the pain for just a few moments or an hour. Until Jesus can get his next $1.80 to buy another temporary fix. I wasn't willing to give him what he needed. Maybe he was afraid to ask. It is easier in most cases to get someone to part with some change than it is to see a person affect real change by digging deep into their hearts and their pockets to meet the need that an individual standing in front of them so obviously and screamingly displays—even when there aren't the words to
frame . . .

. . . their obvious need.

I'm guilty.

I'm guilty of treating Jesus like shit. And I'm guilty of ignoring his requests for some change.

Change please!

I'm not comfortable with change.

He continually asks me for change—and I tend to look the other way and pretend that he doesn't exist so I can continue on in the direction I'm heading—I don't know what the other path may hold and I don't want to be told that I may be going the wrong way.

He asks me for change and I look past him or through him and hope that he and his request will fade into a distant memory so that I can continue to meet my needs while I ignore his.

Yes—what I do to the least of these or what I don't do for the least I do to him. The one who freely gave me everything. The one who was willing to lay his life down in exchange for mine.

It would seem that Terrence McNally came to this realization long before I did. He is a bold and brave man. He must have known that God not only doesn't hate fags but that it was important to use his gifts as a writer to create a powerful piece of art that would speak the outrageous language of his tribe to invite them into a relationship with the one who loved them passionately, profoundly and for all eternity. I am only speculating—I have no idea what Terrence McNally's beliefs are. But I would have to guess that something about the Jesus story resonated with him. Something compelled him to present the Gospel as good news to a group of people who could only hear it as pure judgment surrounded by hellfire and God's vengeful wrath. But he would have to get their attention, so they would be able to hear it.

Mr. McNally obviously poured himself into the production and was confident that this piece would be revolutionary, and it seems he hoped that there would be open arms on the other side of the curtain—arms that would embrace the most beautiful message and maybe even embrace the messenger who was bold enough to tell something so outrageous in a most outrageous way.

Because that is what Jesus did.

But first, he had to get the attention of a hardened group of people—people who had pretty much figured God out and understood him so well that they would fight wars in his name. They would stone those who didn't quite believe in the same way—and crucify those who would forever upset the balance that they had so desperately fought to keep.

So Jesus showed up—for all intents and purposes as a bastard child two thousand years– (give or take a few) before HBO or Showtime. A time when divorce and infidelity were punishable by death. And suddenly this religious group of people who were so concerned about every piece of food they would eat—every fabric that would touch their skin—every appearance they would make in the temple—were now somehow supposed to buy the fact that their long-awaited Messiah was a bastard son of a dumb carpenter and his teenage wife who didn't even have the decency to plan a proper birth for the one who would bring life to all who were willing to believe?

And even if they had been able to swallow that, they would never buy into the teachings of a guy who was unwilling to obey the basic laws of the Sabbath—how in the hell could this man be God when he continually chose to over-ride the very rules he had put in place thousands of years before? Rules and laws that these religious men spent a lifetime perfecting, preaching and enforcing—sparing no expense and sparing no one who would get in their way.

To top it all off, Jesus had a new message—it was a message not of rules and laws and dictates but a message of unconditional love and grace. He turned the tables of the temple over and he pissed off the priests when he called them slippery snakes and decorated tombs that reeked of death on the inside no matter how ornate the outsides were. No matter how pious they could appear.

This was a man—a bastard—in their eyes—who had no credentials. He had no right to teach this blasphemous message and he certainly had no right to be healing the sick or forgiving men of their sins. This was unconscionable and unheard of and they would not tolerate it. *Bring the heretic in!!!*

This message not only went against everything they were trained to believe but the messenger could not be more unorthodox and unappealing to the power structure of the religious time.

Kill the messenger.
Kill the bastard!
(We are running out of time!)

The funny thing is—the regular people loved him. His message was for the hookers and the lepers and the misunderstood. The messenger was from the outside and he spoke the language of his tribe. And his message was good news. It was a message of love and it was a message of hope. It was exactly the message the world longed for but didn't believe possible. And suddenly the guy who worked with wood, would shatter everything that the religious believed and validate everything that the irreligious could only dream—and he did it all on his small stage—off off off Broadway to a small but receptive audience . . . and a few dangerous protestors.

Needless to say, I went back to see the show a number of times and I always took a friend or twelve to see the show. I wanted as many people as possible to witness this unusual presentation of the Gospel so I could selfishly listen in on their thoughts and reactions to this unholy spectacle.

One particular night I brought a beautiful friend who was recently married and had a child on the way. Although he is gay-friendly, I knew that he was also of the opinion that Jesus can change anyone willing to be changed. So I thought it would be interesting to hear what he had to say after seeing the play.

My heart began to race as we neared the final scene—the crucifixion where the actor playing Jesus is stripped to his small white briefs and wrapped in pink and purple chiffon—and nailed to a humiliating tree.

I won't give the ending away but I will say that it is the most powerful presentation of Jesus I have ever seen in my entire life—and I've been to about 40,000 church services and passion plays. As Jesus stands before the crowd, and as the actors begin to gather at his feet, as the depth and beauty of the Jesus message begins to become crystal clear to the audience members and as eyes around the darkened stage are quickly filling with pools of tears—my friend Ian jumped out of his seat and ran to the foot of the stage. *(Oh my God Ian, what are you doing . . . what are you doing.)* With reckless abandon and utter humility, Ian leapt up on the stage and fell on his face at the feet of Jesus where he wept loudly and kissed the actor's bare feet.

I was horrified. Oh my GOD Ian what are you doing? Don't you realize how foolish this display makes me look? These actors know that I brought you here tonight. Oh my God.

Oh My God.

It was then that I realized that I too, had wanted to leap on the stage the first two or three times I had witnessed this presentation. I came so close to running up to the stage the first night I was there . . . almost surprised that everyone in the audience wasn't doing the same thing. But over time, after hearing the message a few times and becoming accustomed to the emotion, I now acted with healthy "adult" reserve. My God, what had I been thinking? I would have looked so foolish.

I would have completely made a scene.

As Ian continued to weep at Brandon's feet—holding them and kissing them, over and over pouring love and passion and generally making a big teary mess—Brandon, the young gay man playing Jesus began to weep. Uncontrollably. Right there on that stage.

I later learned that Brandon hadn't really been a believer in this Jesus story, he had taken the part because it sounded like a challenge. But he said that the experience that night forever changed his life. He could feel something bigger than himself—a power and love that transcended the play or the stage—that allowed him, for a moment in time, to encounter the holy. To taste of the divine.

And I realized something profound as well. As much as I like to pummel the religious right for being so prideful, arrogant and almost certainly missing the point, I realized I have no right to point my finger at anyone that I deem to be pious, proud and sickeningly judgmental and religious—because I am all of those things and more.

It is only by grace that we are saved.

Through faith.

Faith in an outrageous message—a message of pure authentic love without condition.

A love that has been displayed on the earth's stage time and time again by those willing to lay their lives down for another. For those willing to kneel prostrate at the feet of the one who demands nothing at all. Nothing except the audacity to drop your pretensions and pride and leap up on a stage in front of God and everybody to kiss the feet of Jesus . . . to lie at his feet and weep.

And foolishly, like a child, like Ian—

just believe.

14.5

More Miserable— An A.D.D. Soliloquy

So, the next chapter was going to be the big musical. I mean, what gay book is to be taken seriously without the grandeur and spectacle of an epic musical? This was a big budget production to boot. It would involve a cast of hundreds, intricate period costuming— and YOU were going to be the star—singing the selected lyrics from some of the most moving moments of Broadway. I can almost hear you now! Well, that was until I received this delightful email from the people who represent the author of the lyrics and book for Les Miserables.

> Your request to quote lyrics from Les Miserables in your forthcoming book has been denied. Accordingly you are not authorized to reprint any of the lyrics.
>
> Best regards,
>
> Steve

Do you hear the people type
Typing the words of steadfast men...

This is the music of a people who
will not be generous!

I had politely asked for many months in many different ways if we could secure permission for reprint on just a handful of lyrics.

I mean, less than 150 words from that humongous production—150 words that would be inserted carefully and lovingly into this book of more than 40,000 words. I asked God to provide a miracle—and as the deadline for publication became impossibly close—I asked one last time. I held my breath. Then, just last night on the day before our final deadline, I received the terse reply. I was devastated. It was a little like Dorothy finally reaching the Emerald City and her request to meet the Wizard was met with a brusque

"THE WIZARD ISN'T IN!"
(And the portal slams shut!)

Now what?

This was the big musical. The key to the entire book. I would have been happy to pay some sort of licensing fees, just to have the chance to hear you sing along with the moving anthems and heart-breaking timeless refrains.

Then I remembered the wise words of Sarah Silverman: "When God gives you AIDS, and he does give you AIDS—make Lemon-AIDS!"

So in a moment I had the solution. There are no copyright laws about humming! I could hint at the lyrics, remind you of the scene and you could all hum super quietly at home.

No harm, no foul.

Because the show must go on!

And this is one humdinger of a show. And you are the hum/singer of the show. . .

So for God's sake, don't print or sing any of the lyrics. Just hum. And enjoy some freshly-squeezed lemonAids!

Ho hum!

15.
Les(s)
Miserable(s).

Finding the **key** to enable us all
to be **less miserable.**
Gay, straight and everything in between.

Through Sublime Subversion

The sounds of the ocean crashing on Table Rock just outside our bedroom window on the sun-soaked South Laguna beach let me know that heaven was in reach on that exquisite morning. I knew I had a few more minutes before *Shews*™—our very verbal pit bull/boxer mix—would begin telling me through his eerily close attempts at English that it was time for our leisurely morning walk. I could hear the rhythmic breathing of the man I loved with all my heart—the man I love even though we're now apart. And it was my birthday.

As I was lying there thinking about nothing in particular, God interrupted my thoughts, as he sometimes would. I don't claim to hear voices in my head—just distinct impressions—thoughts that I wouldn't have on my own. Thoughts that usually came from left field, and most pushed me from my comfort zone. (Like, "Go ask your neighbor if he is considering suicide." But that's a story from a whole different chapter in another book altogether.)

Kyle had bought us tickets to see *Les Miserables*—my favorite Broadway performance—in celebration of the revolution of my birth. (I'm French, bear with me, subversion runs through my veins.) I had seen the show years before, but I was looking forward to seeing it just the same. Suddenly out of the relative silence—sans the sound of the surf pounding the soft sands, and the soft snoring of Ky and *Shews*™ (in a breathy harmony)—I knew God was trying to speak to me.

"Tonight I want you to pay close attention to the show. There is a key to be found and it is a key that will start the revolution and it is a key you need to know." My heart began to race. Now I was no longer going for pure enjoyment. I was on a mission. And I knew that he wanted me to see something, to understand something that would be essential for this book. So on that July morning, as I walked the canine formerly known as *Cash* . . . who became *Cashew*—now *Shews*™ my heart raced at the prospect of discovering something sublime and new.

(I'm playing stage manager: Here are your hints/cues:)
This is the number where the ensemble asks if you can
hear the people singing—singing those songs from very
angry men... Start humming...GO!

For years I could hear the people sing and they were angry. I was angry. Who wouldn't be angry—after a lifetime of being misunderstood, a lifetime of being judged, a lifetime of hell—where you are told over and over that you can only look forward to an eternity of *hell* . . . basically more of the same. Only longer, and even hotter than Southern California in July. Wow. What a shame.

Curtain Call

As I watched the show that night I was swept away in the grandeur of it all. And even as tears came—so did the revelation that would spark the revolution. Jean Valjean was a man who committed a very minor crime. It was a crime of survival—and it was for the survival of another—little Cosette—another victim needing only a morsel of bread to survive. A bit of nourishment to thrive. So he took some bread to help a helpless and poverty-stricken child. And that was all it took for the law to come down hard. And for the rest of Valjean's life he would be permanently scarred:

2 4 6 0 1

He was reduced to a number. No longer a name.

Just as you are no longer a person.

But merely a FAG.

In *Les Miserables* Jean Valjean committed a minor crime in order to survive. Under the law, he would always be a criminal, a number, an enemy of the state. He ran his entire life from his accuser, despite the fact that he had changed. But a personal battle continued until his accuser no longer remained.

It is the same in this revolution played out in life, like on the stage. We are all being accused by the specter of death for the crimes of survival many of us have committed. Some were inflicted on us, some we've brought on ourselves, but the results are all the same. We keep running, we keep dying, all the while we keep lying . . .

. . . to hide the things that keep us enslaved.

We are being hunted and hounded by the avenger of blood and his greatest weapon is our own unnecessary shame and the secrets that we hold safe, locked inside our brain. Will we continue to run and continue to hide while we mask the mountains of our pain, hidden deep within our pride?

(We hide behind the coolest new cell phones, expensive cars and exclusive brand names—so you will judge what we have—not who we are.)

Javert was the law. And he was hell-bent on making Valjean pay for the tiny crime that he committed way, way back in the day. Even after Valjean had served years and years in hard labor— Javert was still tormented by Jean Valjean's gross sin—so he spent the rest of his life trying to bring him back in. Trying desperately to let him know that he would never be free.

Or, free of him.

In that dark theater I began to see it all. Javert was the church—the long arm of the law—the pious pope and the preachers claw. And my brothers and sisters who happened to be queer, were the ones who broke a single law—and now were living in abject fear. Running from Javert. Running from law.

And running from what, they were told, was a very angry God.

So Javert continued to pursue. And no matter how much good Valjean would do—Javert would not relent. Despite the fact that Valjean's life had been redeemed and he lived his years quite well— Javert, at every turn makes his existence a never ending chase and a living hell.

Reminding him of the never ending hell—

(Coming soon to an eternity near you!)

In the casting call of this real life production of *The Miserable*—it seems that many Christians have been relishing their role as Javert.

Committing a litany of sins of their own, but spending all their time telling their gay brothers and sisters that they are not welcome at home.

And so we roam.

(Roaming charges do apply—and quickly multiply.)

But the show must go on . . .

As the story builds and the great standoff scene unfolds—where Javert swears he will get retribution—that Valjean will never escape his wrath—there is the promise of a very real blood bath.

Javert screams from his pulpit.

(Turn or BURN!)

And Valjean shouts back.

(We're here. We're queer. Get used to it!)

But no one is listening and there is only a great deal of noise. The battle merely escalates . . . and still we are losing so many precious boys.

> *Stage manager here again: This is that killer song toasting those pretty boys who went to our heads and the witty boys who actually went to our beds—this is a toast to them, and a toast to you!*

The revolution has been raging and so much blood has been shed. Memories of those we have loved and are no longer—those who should be living—but now are dead. So many of God's precious children left bleeding and dying alongside the road.

Even God cries. He really does, you know.

And yet the shouting continues.
The anger stokes the fiery flames and the more laws that are
passed, the more who will be gassed . . .

. . . in one way or another.

It's all the same. Such a shame.

When I think of all the potential, all the love, and all the lives that
have been lost . . . this has been a whole new holocaust. Although I
may offend many or a few—because I have no idea what it was
like to have been a Jew—

under Hitler's heinous regime—

I know it is the same brand of hate that has been causing so many
to die—or at the very least, live out their dark and desolate lives,
hiding in the closet ghetto or in their open-air gay ghetto—waving
rainbow flags.

The marginalization is all the same.

*Humming Cue: This is that line in the final refrain refer-
ring to the music of a people who are adamant—they will
never be slaves again!*

And we must not be slaves again. Either to prejudices, judgment or
hate—or even to our own wretched sin—the stuff that keeps us all
in chains—addictions, conflictions or promiscuity leading to se-
vere afflictions—

Will you join in that fight—the fight that will give us the right—

The rite that will set you free?

Then it happens. Right there on the stage—right before our eyes. The secret sung in the perfect—key.

Cue Marius: Here you are humming with all of your heart—as Eponine lies dying before you; You are letting her know that if there were any way you could heal her wounds with your words of love, you would. . .

Now, go falsetto on my ass and pull off the gorgeous response from Ponine—the response where all she asks of Marius is to be held, to be sheltered and comforted in her final moments—those moments in the rain.

Blood is covering the barricades separating us from them, and when Javert (the law) is captured by the young bleeding revolutionaries, Valjean is given the chance of a lifetime—a chance to finally be free. He is instructed by the students to kill his arch enemy. In fact—it's his responsibility.

Mercy. (killing)

Mercy for Javert.

Mercy for you.

And mercy for me.

Mercy me.

Mercy and forgiveness are the only key . . . to sublimeSubversion and a life lived in true peace and harmony.

Valjean—who has every right to shoot his nemesis, his lifelong enemy—the man who has made his life an endless chase—the man who caused so much potential to go to waste . . .

. . . is now deserving of a brutal bullet to the head.

(It's not just a good idea, it's the law of the revolution.)

But Valjean knows that this will only make him guilty of another, more heinous crime than stealing bread—way back in time.

And he must also know that those who live by the sword will ultimately die by the sword. So he becomes a hero and so much more. And he does so in a moment:

He *forgives*.

And as a result, Javert lives.

But not for long. The madness overtakes him. How is it possible that this 24601 is actually a man—a man with a heart who could forgive and a man who would let a judgmental, maniacal tyrant live.

(And Javert jumps from a very high bridge.)

Forgiveness breaks the cycle of abuse. It begins to set the captives free and more than anything else—it is healing for you and healing for me. Mainly, we will not die from the bitterness within. And we will rise above the hating bigot's sin. And although we may have broken some tiny law—from a long time ago—we are living out the great command. The most important of all the commands.

To love.
Jesus said so himself.
That the greatest law of all—the law of above all laws is to love.
Well.

Never judge. Lest you be judged.
Only love. Lest you be loved.
And you will.
If you can simply forgive. And live.

It is down to one final dawn, one final day...
One day more! *(It's ok kids, we can legally use song titles.
Just hum along as if it were a lyric)*

(and now you are truly free . . . indeed.)

When we join the revolution, a revolution of forgiveness born of love, we will achieve the goal of ultimate redemption, as we sing boldly in that same refrain . . .

*This is that epic ensemble anthem—the rousing number
that promises the audience that change will happen when
our heartbeats match the drumbeats and a new life will
actually start when tomorrow finally comes! (Are we still
humming along?)*

And that life will be lived in love and shared with those in so much need with so much pain. And when we give of ourselves, and pour ourselves out we will find this revolution will begin. For each of us, personally, and for all of society. But it would cost us all our lives—if our God himself, had not already paid the price.

Jean Valjean then belts out that heartbreaking refrain—where he begs God for his adopted son's life. He bargains—offering to die instead. If only he will allow this precious boy to live . . .

For Jean Valjean, redemption does come in the end. It can be owned for now, for the moment and the 525,600 minutes that follow in each subsequent year. (Different stage, but same idea.) And the redemption is owned, not rented or leased, and will carry us just as he carries us, to a place of exquisite rest and authentic peace.

*Do you hear the people sing?
Again, it's ok, you can hum a song title. . .*

Revolution . . . real revolution begins

when we are willing to forgive. In truth, there is nothing we can do about how others have chosen to live. And how their choices have caused us so much pain. But in that act of forgiveness (free of judgment) you can join that last refrain.

For the blood of the One who was without sin has washed your sin away.

A brand new beginning.
A **Love**Revolution

For those with eyes to see, let them see. For those with ears to hear, let them hear. This is a call for revolution and a call for the freedom fighters that make revolutions a reality. It only takes a single decision—a decision to forgive.

And a decision to believe.

That decision can be made at any time, but

Final stage manager cues:
(Here comes the tricky part—but it is so worth it as it is the big finale!)

What the hell, start singing... I don't care anymore. There is no more time to hum... Sing about how Tomorrow may actually be far away . . .

Sing how tomorrow really is the Judgment Day

Remind yourself and everyone in earshot that tomorrow we may discover what God in heaven above may have in store . . .

This is it! There is only one more dawn

Just one more day—that is all...
Just
One
Day More!

Let the Revolution begin!

And let it be sung . . .
And let it be lived . . .
In that perfect key . . .

The key of—Forgive.

Forgive and it shall be forgiven.
Now that is *real* life. And this is real living.

(A sobering A.D.D Aside)

The fact that fags are forgiving Christians will
drive them all insane—just as Valjean's act of
forgiveness for Javert did the same. I can hear
the pious now—"What do you mean you
forgive us? You're the sinners and everyone
knows that God hates fags . . . get away from
our church, away from our children—you in
your filthy rags."

Then the great finale. "We will see you in
hell!"

And won't it be a big surprise—the day after
judgment, in a land of all flies—as they
unpack their devotionals—getting all settled
in—the flames singing their perfectly coiffed
hair.

When they look around smugly—looking
even more ugly—

Only to discover—we are not there.

(P.S. So I haven't completely learned this lesson of forgiveness.
Forgive me. Then forgive them—it's a never ending battle. But so
worth it in the end.)

(P.P.S. There will always be challenges and bitterness is such a natural human response. But even when you get a negative reply from
those lovely folks who own the lyrics from Les Miz—it is so much
better to simply forgive. And find a way to hum yourself back—
rather than launch an attack. And no matter what—please continue
to support that incredible show. Maybe one day the people who
wrote it will listen to the message and quite possibly even grow. It
is a journey, you know.)

16.
Judgment-
Day

You. God.

Judgment Day. What a daunting thought. More frightening than a tax audit. More unsettling than a Senate hearing, lawsuit deposition, religious inquisition or even an intervention. "Hi I'm James and I'm an alcoholic." This is that final day where you stand naked and cowering before the wrath of an angry God—where there will be hell to pay for all the things you've done wrong. And for many of us, that list will be long.

I mentioned in the table of contents, "You are going to have to wait and see on this one." And that may be the truest thing I have written. Nobody knows for sure what that last day will hold as we stand naked, and alone, in front of our pure and sinless God.

If you are a fag, you have been told over and over how sinful you are. You have heard nothing but sermon after sermon laced with anger and hate from all sorts of preachers and pastors and angry smug bastards who somehow have become jury and judge—letting us all know of that long and painful road we will have to trudge.

That road to perdition.

But if you can remember back to chapter 7—sin isn't such a daunting thing. It just means missing the mark. In missing the mark we are not hitting God's perfect plan—that idea he first intended when he created man. Hell, Adam missed the mark right out of the gate. And that wasn't his fault, it was Eve's mistake.

Maybe he should have made Adam and Steve. Women. They can be so tricky! (I hope you know I'm kidding.)

And truthfully, the very people who keep screaming at us about our sin are missing the mark in a thousand different ways. The difference is, they are not gay.

But the bottom line is this: We ALL will miss the mark until our dying day. In my last breath I may be coveting Vicodin® and a fifth of bourbon. (To dull the pain.)

I have been nervous about writing this chapter. I am not God and I have no idea what he has in store. And I also know that this is the last chapter I get to write—and these will be the final words I leave with you—the words that will end this portion of our journey together—so I want these words to be perfect and true.

As I have been rolling this subject over in over in my mind—I realized last night that as the reader approaches Judgment Day—he will undoubtedly be asking, *So I've read almost 151 pages and I still don't know if you think being gay is a sin or not.*

Then it hit me.

It doesn't matter.

Not whether being gay is a sin or not—but it doesn't matter what I think.

It only matters what God thinks. And although I can't begin to imagine everything that God thinks—(even God changes his mind from time to time . . . like when he changed the essential dietary laws that I mentioned in the Peter Vision. God knows, he may have done it again.) One thing I have discovered on this journey is that it is not always all black and white.

Ultimately, this will be a decision you have to make.

I believe God has a special path for each of his sons and daughters. And when it comes to Judgment Day we will be naked and alone as we approach this glorious loving God who may or may not be sitting on a throne. He may be barefoot sitting on the grass. Who knows?

But instead of meeting a God of wrath . . .

I know this for a fact.

You will stand face to face, for the very first time in your life—

with **Pure
Love**.

You will be overwhelmed by the fact that you are loved. You will be leveled by this force of love and it will leave you breathless and addicted, wanting more. It will be the greatest high you've ever known and it will be the first time in your life that you have ever felt at home. Because all your life—you have been displaced. You have never, ever felt that you belong. And there is a reason for that. God has created you to not fit into the system that we have known, because he has created your true and lasting home.

An incredible place where you no longer need to roam. (And that place can be here—right where you are because Jesus said the Kingdom of God is now. And when I live in that perfect place of rest—where I learn to love myself and put my fear and loathing on the shelf. It can be heaven NOW.)

And all those words of judgment that you have heard screamed at you for your entire life—will be simply washed away—they will be eradicated in his perfect light.

It will be glorious and like nothing Hollywood could ever paint on a shimmering, silver screen—no matter how big the budget. No matter the director. It is beyond your wildest dreams.

And mine.

Perfect love—casts out all fear. And on that final day as you stand in the presence of that perfect love, the last thing you will feel . . .

. . . is queer.

In a moment, in a twinkling of an eye, you will be transformed. All the things you would have changed about yourself—your weight, your selfishness, your hate, your anger, your jealousy, your pettiness and greed, even the grand canyon of your fucking need. All of it will be wiped away. The emptiness will be filled. The old man will be killed and there in that moment a new man will come to life. And this new man—this brand new YOU—will hear these words.

Well done—well done—my good and faithful friend. You didn't quit, you held out to the end. And the things that were broken—the things that were torn—are now the things that I will mend.

And all of this happens in an instant in the presence of his perfect love.

But then the hellish voice returns.

Oh, listen to this deluded man talk about love, love, love. What about the fact that scripture is quite clear. There will be a day of Judgment and sinners will have to pay for the things they've done and the people they've laid.

I'm so sorry—I guess you missed it.

You clearly haven't paid attention. Or you couldn't believe there would be such divine intervention . . .

That day has already come.

The price has been paid.

Hell sent out the invoice and God himself saved the day.

No matter how many times the proud and pious have heard the sermons—they don't seem to put the pieces together. Judgment has already come—the sins of all mankind are now under the blood.

God cared enough to send the very best—that is the hallmark of our faith. He sent his beloved Son to stand naked and alone.

Right there out in the open. Right there, in our place.

And even though he was sinless. Even though he wasn't gay. He became gay for you. And the price has now been paid.

In full.

He was brutalized and beaten by the religious men of his day—sure they turned him over to the Romans to do the dirty work—but they set the wheels in motion to have this gentle lover of all mankind, humiliated, beaten and bleeding—beyond recognition—on this long, long road to perdition—a road you no longer have to take. It's a simple decision that you can make.

If you can believe it, your debt has been paid.

Jesus took your place. He offered you life, he offered you peace, he washed you clean, and love emanates from his face.

He's madly in love with you. He really is, you know.

He was your stand-in, your stunt double in that very first passion play. It was the role of a lifetime and the role cost him his life.

He was standing in for you, and standing in for me—when the nine-inch nails of judgment pierced his flesh and crushed his bones—blood caked and crusted on his heaving body on that wretched stake—but instead of feeling hate—he even took their place . . .

As he struggled for his final breaths, he used those breaths to fuel the thing that he would do next . . . he looked his tormentors in the eyes and he chose to love.

And forgive.

He forgave them. He forgave me. And he has forgiven you. He even forgives the ones who have been turning the religious screws to make our lives a living hell. The ones who say they love Jesus well—but they don't care much for you.

It all happened on that horrific day.

Complete separation from the love of his father as he carried the weight of all of our sins—on his shoulders. On a tree. Alone. As he gasped his final breaths, blood, love, spit and sweat mingled and poured out for all to see.

And this judgment day took care of our debt—and has set the captive free.

So when someone tells you that God Hates Fags—you can know in an instant that you are talking to the father of lies, because that God does not exist. Just the opposite—you are a treasure in your Father's eyes. So much so that he was willing to die.

For you.

For me.

And anyone foolish enough to believe.

What kind of fool believes?

Only a fool

for Christ's sake.

Judgment Day. It is not something you have to dread any longer. Nor do you need to worry about anyone else's sin—not even your own. Because God himself paid the price—there's no greater love that could be shown.

So—what about this gay thing? For those of you for whom the question still remains . . .

The chorus of the pious won't seem to go away . . .

The answer is quite simple. You are now judge and jury—and by your decision, you can miss hell's fury. You hold the verdict in your very own hands. Your debt has been paid. Already. By the God who became man.

Believe it.

Or not.

Live in that freedom—be free of your demons and put your hands in the hand of the One who loves you the most. It's a long journey. If there is anything he wants you to change—I'm sure *he* will let you know.

(He is Jewish, remember.)

I am absolutely sure that not even death or life
can separate us from God's love.

Not even angels or demons,
the present or the future,
or any powers can do that.

Not even the highest places or the lowest,
or anything else in all creation can do that.
Nothing at all can ever separate us from God's love

Because of what
Christ Jesus our Lord has done

—Romans 8:38-39 (NIRV)

Raised from the
Deadication.

What will you be wearing on Judgment Day?

(Let's hope it's before Labor Day—or you won't be wearing white!)

The thought of writing this book scared the hell out of me. I've been a pretty bad Christian and a fairly decent homo for a very long time. But the idea that these two wildly disparate worlds may merge seemed about as likely as Grey Goose sponsoring the Southern Baptist convention. It wasn't possible. Or so I thought.

For the weeks, months and years that I wrestled with the idea of putting these words to paper (eight long years, to be exact) I must have asked God about 50 thousand times, "Is this book your idea or am I living in Satan's perfect will?" I even put this manuscript down for over three years, because I was living in abject fear.

Then for a few weeks, I put my doubts on hold. I started writing and the words exploded. But the giant question marks remained.

I remember sitting in LAX, waiting to board my flight to the East Coast when in a moment of tangible desperation, I asked God to give me a sign that would irrefutably prove to me that this was his dream and not mine. I mean, really. Who wants to be a gay activist for God? The artist formerly known for hating fags?

As I took my aisle seat, with my overpriced Starbucks sandwich in hand, I remember feeling a bit of excitement as I watched a cool-looking rock star slip into the middle seat next to me. He smiled as he pointed out our matching sandwiches. This flight looked promising.

But before I could introduce myself to the intriguing young musician, a slightly annoyed accountant type interrupted our about-to-start conversation to point out that I may be in the wrong seat. I was supposed to be across the aisle. Damn bean counters, always sticklers for detail. Why would it matter if he sat in this seat, or the one across the aisle?

And then, it all became clear.

To my horror, I noticed that the middle seat across the way was filled, and I mean filled, with a large older woman in a once brightly-colored muu muu. This could be Maui's own Delta Dawn. A horrifying, dead lei drooped around her sagging neck and she was mysteriously pulling French fries from deep inside her muu muu somewhere between her legs. As I reluctantly took my new seat, her gray, grinch-like gravity-defying hair invaded my Soviet air space. I leaned as far to my right as I possibly could without falling out of my seat. I longed to be back in my old seat next to the rock star . . . sharing our matching sandwiches and swapping witty repartee. Who knows what else we may have in common. What if we both hated mayonnaise?

As I slumped back into my seat, closing my eyes for that magical moment where the wheels lift from the earth, I distinctly heard God's distressing words.

"This is my special daughter. Honor her."

Shit. Why are God's special kids always dressed like homeless Hawaiians?

I gave this odd woman a weak smile. "Pepsi?" I asked in my incredibly lame attempt at honoring this disheveled woman who was continually rummaging through a million crinkly shopping bags arranged all about her feet. I so wished that Piggly Wiggly hadn't given her the option of paper or plastic.

"There," I thought. "My work here is done. I offered her a drink. I smiled. I was warm."

Now back to me.

The flight was uneventful. I noticed the rock star had fallen asleep, so with my iPod in place, I tried to do the same.

Hours later the captain announced that we would be landing soon. Although I normally keep to myself for most of the flight, this is usually my cue to politely converse because there is no way now to be trapped in an endless exchange about grandchildren, Amway, or worse.

Before I could come up with a good conversation starter, my neighbor interrupted my thoughts. "So what do you do?" (It would seem that she had the same system.)

I told her I write books. Suddenly we launched into a great little dialogue and she asked if I had any copies so she could take a look. I pulled out *God.com* and *God.net* and placed them in her hands. She froze and stared at the books for what seemed like an eternity. After several awkward minutes I got up and left her alone in her motionless state. I was worried she might think I was giving her the copies, but I couldn't as they were destined for someone on the other coast. And I didn't have any more. So I schmoozed with flight attendants and tried to kill some time. When I returned I noticed she was still holding the books. Still staring directly at them. It appeared as if she had slipped into a waking coma.

"Oh my God," I said. "I didn't mean for you to have to hold those this entire time."

She finally looked up and locked eyes with me. "I don't mind. I have paged through and read bits here and there . . . "

And then it happened. This strange woman began to morph before my eyes and I sensed the presence of greatness as she became like the oracle in the Matrix, speaking words of truth. The only thing missing were the chocolate chip cookies.

"These are not your words, my son. These are God's words. You didn't write these books, God did. Am I right?"

I was dumbstruck.

"I am so sorry. So sorry." Her head dropped in shame. "I was supposed to engage you hours ago . . . and I'm sorry for judg . . . " She stopped short. All the while I was thinking she was homeless, she was undoubtedly thinking I was some dumb fag. I was wearing low rider jeans, combat boots and a black sleeveless t-shirt. Because I was so taken by her strange get-up I didn't realize how strange I must have looked to her.

The very real problem of **Homelessexuality**

She continued to shake her head. "I could have learned so much from you. I wish I had been more aware. I'm sorry my son. I'm so terribly sorry."

I looked at her in total disbelief. "Actually, it's me that owes you an apology. I am guilty of the same. God told me that you are a special daughter and I was supposed to honor you but my attempts were extremely lame."

She smiled. "It's okay. We're talking now. And I have something important to say so hear me well. You have been called to reach a group of people that no one else is reaching. These books were only a start. But God is calling you to the edge, isn't he?" She didn't wait for my response. She didn't need to, she already knew.

"And you are afraid, aren't you? You must do what God is calling you to do. No one else is. You have been called for such a time as this to reach some of God's special kids. So much damage has been done . . . so much damage. You are called, my son to reach this group. You know the language and the terrain. Do not fear, be strong and courageous . . . for this is God's doing. Not yours."

Tears filled my eyes. I couldn't even speak. I nodded and looked her deeply in the eyes.

She touched my shoulder and within a split second I could feel God there all over me like a warm waterfall. This stranger in the big tent dress had a direct line to God and I knew that the words coming out of her mouth were not her own. They were his.

She spoke a brief blessing or prayer over me. I can't remember a thing she said, I can only remember tears pouring down my cheeks and the feeling that I wish she would never stop. I wanted to spend hours with this woman I had tried so hard to get away from, but we had touched the ground and the double bells indicated it was time to leave. It felt as though I had visited heaven, but now must come back to earth.

The rock star left, but I didn't notice.

"I am so sorry, but I don't even know your name." I reached out my hand for hers.

"Twyla. So nice to meet you."

"Nice to meet you too, I'm James." God then told me a few things about Twyla—and I shared them with her.

She smiled and tears now filled her eyes. I realized that this was God's special daughter, a princess, an angel, a treasure. He didn't see the muu muu. Only the tender heart.

When you think about it, fashions are fickle—they come, they go, they fade, like the flowers around Twyla's neck. Even our bodies are just muu muus of flesh . . .

that will one day droop and die away.

But it's the soul that remains.

"I am a switchboard operator at a maximum security prison. I try to share love with the guards so they in turn can share love with their wards. I'm seeing miracles take place every day! Before that, I worked in an armory. God sure works in mysterious ways."

She hugged me hard, taking me in to her heart—the dead lei crushed against my cheek. I didn't want that hug to ever end. And although I suspected it before, I now knew for certain that God has most unusual friends.

Angels do fly.

And some without wings. Instead of carrying golden harps they may be carrying plastic things.

I hope I'm never again distracted by rock stars or am put off by bad fashion. In this case the price would have been too high and I would have missed God's heart and fiery passion. And I would not have known for certain just how much God must love fags. Or he never would've spoken to me so clearly through a most unlikely woman, his precious daughter in a muu muu—with a thousand crinkly bags.

Thank you Twyla,
this book is dedicated to you.

Acknowledgments

Nature abhors a vacuum. And so do I–they suck.

(And I'm not talking about the Hoover™ that I was forced to push around the house when I was a kid – although I hate those vacuums too.)

I'm talking about the kind of vacuums that exist because someone isn't willing to do what they were called or created to do. Especially when so many beautiful sons and daughters suffer as a result.

There has been a great big-ass vacuum left in our world because of abject fear. I was almost sucked into that hollow void myself – and would never have put these words to paper if it were not for some incredible warriors of light – friends who would not let me put this crazy manuscript down until it was complete. And for that, I remain deeply grateful.

There are no words that will ever adequately express the depth of the gratitude I feel for all of you – so forgive my simple "Thank You" and know that one day, looking from eternity backwards – we may all be able to celebrate together – a great big "Gay Bash" with God's brilliant, sensitive and beautiful kids who chose to ignore ignorant words like "God Hates Fags" and embrace the God of love – the God who loved so damn much that he actually gave everything . . . to the very last drop . . . to show his love in a tangible way. All I can say is a very naked "Thanks."

To Andrea White (your artistry in my life has gone everywhere—including the gorgeous cover for this book), Anthony Annibale, Tommy Hall, Norm, Jeremy Casper, Sam Sparro, Ryan Leebrick, Aaron Gautschi and Jim Standridge (my amazing straight friend who read the manuscript and responded – "Now I wish I were gay!!" Man, Jimmy, you are a saint!) You are some of the best friends anyone could ever hope to have. Thank you for risking so much in your own journeys of "believe." There were days I don't think I would have made it through without you.

Thank you Chris and Karyn Falson for the years of friendship, wise counsel, selfless giving, and reckless drinking that helped take the edge off – when there was far more edge than any of us would have liked. You will forever be my partners in crime.

To all those who read the early versions of these words and gave your incredible feedback to make this ring with more authenticity, I can only say thanks. (Even if you wished I had toned it down, or whether or not you agreed with me! I loved being challenged to find out what I truly did believe.)

Thank you . . . Kyle Pierce (This is turning out to be a beautiful, ". . . And Everything After" Mmmmmhhhh!) Paul G, and Double G. Steve Keller (You were a pivotal game changer for me and your authentic love enabled me to write like the wind.) James Bowen, James Brandon (for putting your career on hold while you put yourself on the cross for so many years and so many audiences) and Asian James (my bi-anxious friend who lives a life of service and love). Thank you Lisa Darden, Chiara Tellini, Frank Marquette, Brad Jersak, my crazy identical twin half-sister Kelly, Rowland Nativel, Shea Blackston, Mark Tarbox and Steve and Becky Knight (for all your tireless giving and sacrifices you have made to help so many of God's favorite kids!)

Thank you David Kopp. You have been a rock star and advocate. This book may not have seen the light of day without you.

Thank you Rachelle for challenging me on the content for over ten months before you signed on as my agent. And thank you for jumping in and editing this brilliantly and with so much finesse. You were hand selected and divinely so. I remain in awe of your gifts and more importantly—your heart.

To Christian de la Huerta – there are no words that will do justice to the gratitude I feel for all you have taught me over this past year. Through your workshops, retreats and the power of the breathwork – I have been forever changed. Living a life of reaction will now be a thing of the past. Thank you for the years you have poured out to so many all over the world in your books, in your non-egoic manner and in the way you model love in the very fabric of your everyday life. (And thank you for opening the door to Findhorn Press! We had to go all the way to the northeast coast of Scotland to get this baby in print.)

Speaking of print–thank you Thierry Bogliolo–the best and most selfless, loving Head of Publishing I have ever met. Thank you for taking a chance on this crazy little book. I am forever in your debt. (And all the rest of the incredible Findhorn Press team—and especially the posse at IPG!)

Finally, thank you Mom for becoming a new best friend. It has been years in the making and I realize this book could undo much of the progress we've made. But, like I've told you before, this is like insulin. If you are a diabetic it can save your life. If not, it will kill you. Please put this down now and go have some ice cream instead! I love you and remain grateful that you brought me into this world and have helped me laugh all the way through. And what's more – you introduced me to my very best friend. The God of the Universe. With all my heart – thank you.

And to all of you, gay or straight, who are willing to use your talents, voice or heart to awaken the world to the grave injustices that have been done to some of God's beloved kids—thanks. It doesn't feel like enough. But maybe this is a good place to start.

I love you all. Thanks.

FINDHORN PRESS

Life-Changing Books

For a complete catalogue,
please contact:

Findhorn Press Ltd
117–121 High Street
Forres IV36 1AB
Scotland, UK

t +44(0)1309 690582
f +44(0)131 777 2711
e info@findhornpress.com

or consult our catalogue online
(with secure order facility) on
www.findhornpress.com

For information on the Findhorn Foundation:
www.findhorn.org